Command Center Handbook

Proactive IT Monitoring

Protecting Business Value Through Operational Excellence

Abdul A Jaludi

This book is dedicated to the staff who performs day to day functions within a command center. At times it may seem a thankless job, but without their hard work and dedication, 'business as usual' would not be possible.

Table of Contents

Prologue

A massive category 5 hurricane hits the town of Galveston, Texas, early Saturday morning and slowly travels northwest toward Abilene. Winds of 200 mph ravage the state as the storm continues moving northwest. Two days later, on Monday afternoon, a second hurricane—a category four—hits Corpus Christi, Texas, and continues toward New Mexico.

By Tuesday afternoon half of Texas is without power, and the storms continue to wreak havoc over much of the state. By the time the second storm leaves the state and moves into New Mexico, hundreds of lives have been lost, damage is in the billions, and 75% of Texas is without power.

Prior to the arrival of the storms, Online Brands, an Internet-based retailer with headquarters in Texas, had moved operations to their alternate facilities located in California and Georgia. Online order processing continues without any loss of service. The company's CEO, John Montgomery, gets an update from CIO Amanda Blakely saying that the Texas data center has suffered major damage as a result of the hurricane. Though they're saddened by the destruction of the storm, they are relieved that the operations centers relocated the workload to their data centers in other locations. The damaged data center will remain closed in order to allow staff to focus on their families' needs. Customers within the affected area are being giving priority on orders and inventory. No impacts to customers outside of the affected area have been reported.

The headquarters of World Insurance Group is also located in Texas, but its situation is very different. Its generators ran out of fuel and service stations are closed because of power outages, so the main data center has been shut down. The company is unable to process any insurance-related work. New claims processing, claim payments, and sales of new policies, as well as billing, collections, and other company functions, are at a standstill. CEO Frank Mayer has been unable to reach his CIO, Hank Anderson, because of damage to communications within Texas.

On Wednesday morning, Mayer assembles a team and drives to the company's main command center. It is a ghost town. There is no power, and there is visible damage to the building. The team heads to Anderson's home, where they find him and his family trying to salvage what little they can from what used to be their home.

The update Anderson provides to Mayer and the team is not good. Some of the command center staff members were injured, and many face major storm-related damage at home and are unable to help with recovery efforts. Three out of 60 staff members are available to begin recovery efforts and are currently on standby. They are waiting for word from the disaster recovery company on when systems and space will become available. Unfortunately they must wait for higher priority customers to finish before they can begin, which may not happen until full power is restored to the customer sites and priority customers begin to leave the facility.

Anderson contacts FEMA and other government agencies. World Insurance Group is faced with a backlash of angry customers who are unable to file a claim or collect any desperately needed insurance money, so the agencies promise to help. After assessing the situation, plans are formulated to get World Insurance Group operational at a facility in New York within one to two weeks.

On Wednesday morning, Global Financial Holdings CEO Victor G. Capistrano receives a very disturbing call from his division heads. Very important clients in New York and Washington, D.C., as well as in London, Paris, Hong Kong, Singapore, Switzerland, Brazil, and other locations, are threatening to take their business elsewhere if service is not restored soon. They have tried to get in touch with Andrew Cunningham, the head of technology, or his delegate but have had no luck.

Cunningham is on vacation on an African expedition. He has been out of contact with coworkers and is unaware of the situation affecting them. Global Financial has two data centers in Texas, but neither has suffered damage from the hurricanes. Though they lost main utility power, they seamlessly moved onto generator power, leaving all computer systems fully operational. Unfortunately the carriers that supply and manage their communication lines didn't fare as well, and as a result neither data center is able to communicate with anyone or anything beyond its own walls. The company's command center lost power and communication with the outside world as well.

On Thursday morning, the news outlets report that communications will be down for at least two weeks. Mike Silverman, who is filling in for Cunningham and is unaware of the global impact caused by the loss of communications, decides to wait for power and communications to be restored. With the loss of the command centers and their monitoring tools, Silverman and the technology teams are unaware that customers are unable to access the fully operational computers within the isolated data centers.

Three days after the storm, on Thursday afternoon, Silverman gets a visit at home from Capistrano, who becomes furious upon learning that the data center teams are unaware of the outage. Capistrano orders Silverman to restore service ASAP or he'll be fired.

Unable to reach anyone by phone, Silverman drives to key staff members' and managers' homes, picking each up for an emergency meeting. It seems that no one had any idea of the scope of the outage and its far-reaching effects. Silverman postpones an investigation and refuses to allow finger pointing until after service is restored.

The team acknowledges that the failed communication system in Texas has isolated both data centers, which under normal conditions would support each other. After brainstorming for the good part of the day, the staff begins to formulate a plan.

The company has an unused data center in Vermont that was slated to be sold. The space had been a primary data center until all equipment was consolidated at the Texas sites. Using a satellite phone, they call the facility. All communications lines, power feeds, and standby generators are still operational.

The plan is to resume service from the former site by physically moving all critical systems. Working with a company that specializes in moving sensitive computer equipment, they will move all equipment back into the Vermont location, reconfigure it, and resume operations. Assuming all of the technicians who will be needed to perform the reconfigurations are available, they estimate service can be restored within seven to 10 days. Most of the team is pessimistic regarding the timeline, due to the amount of damage in Texas and the ability to get the required systems experts or the transport company moving while under a state of emergency.

With the plan in hand, Silverman calls Capistrano on Friday afternoon and updates him on the system status and the plan they've formulated to restore service. Capistrano gives his approval to begin work, but he knows it is too late. Upon hanging up, he prepares his next phone call to notify the appropriate government agencies of the impending failure of his firm. He knows that once service is restored, there will be mass defections to competitors followed by even more massive lawsuits.

The fictional scenarios above describe situations that arose following landfall of category 4 and 5 hurricanes. But anytime a company loses the ability to perform its job, for whatever reason, there are serious repercussions. In the aftermath of Superstorm Sandy, catastrophic system-wide failures do not seem as unlikely as they once may have.

What should those companies have done differently? How could they have been better prepared? What contingency plans needed to be in place before the storms even formed? The answers to those questions can best be determined, verified, and implemented by a properly configured and managed command center.

Introduction

The Operations Center
(Command Center)

Almost every private company, as well as almost every municipal, state, and federal agency looking to reduce expenses is turning to technology. Within information technology, data centers are areas where large savings can be achieved by consolidating locations and duties. Migrating to centralized locations is one of the best ways to cut expenses without having to make drastic cuts in the workforce.

For data centers, consolidation means savings in real estate expenses, utility fees, telecom (high-speed connections), and what may be one of the biggest expenses: software licensing fees. When computers in various data center locations are moved into one site, dramatic cost savings can be achieved on software that is licensed by location.

Before consolidating data centers and equipment rooms, it is best to consolidate command centers. That allows for centralized management of hardware, a task that makes managing a large data center much more effective.

With older technology, command centers and data centers needed to be housed in close proximity, in the same building or within several hundred feet in a nearby location. That was primarily a requirement because of the system consoles, used to monitor and control computer systems, which required a direct connection to the mainframe computers within the data center.

Advances in technology allowed system consoles to be connected remotely and securely over communications lines, either across the network or through a dedicated network. Those advances eliminated the need to have a command center for each data center. With the freedom to move command centers (where the staff manages and monitors computers) to a remote location away from a data center (where the computer systems and supporting equipment are housed) came the ability to manage and monitor multiple data centers from one remote location.

A command center is more than a place filled with people and walls composed of video monitors. The command center ensures your business is able to provide critical services to your customers, day or night, 365 days a year, if that is what the business demands. Customers who are able to access and perform what they need, when they need it, within posted hours, will be satisfied customers with no need to take their business elsewhere.

Customers faced with constant interruptions or worse yet who lose confidence in your ability to provide high-quality, consistent services, will take their business to your competitor. Reengaging lost customers is a much more expensive task than keeping existing ones satisfied. Dissatisfied customers are more likely to let others know of a bad experience through social media, making it more difficult to recruit new clients. Positive social media sentiment, clients leaving positive remarks regarding your company on their social media accounts, helps you keep existing customers while greatly reducing the cost of engaging new customers.

The cost of an efficient command center is minuscule when compared with how much business would be lost by service disruptions. However, a well-run and efficient command center might cause senior executives to consider budget cuts due to the mistaken perception of a lack of busy work within the walls, which is misleading. The reason service disruptions are low is because the command center is achieving its goal in the best way possible: by preventing them from happening in the first place. Take away resources from the command center, the reason your applications were always available, and you are likely to start losing customers due to an increase in service disruptions. That cause and effect may not always be apparent because command center senior management rarely advertises resource reductions and may not be aware of the corresponding customer losses.

Contrary to popular belief, the main purpose of the command center is not to fix problems as they occur, but to prevent them from happening. Think about what happens when there's a fire in a building. You may put out the fire and save the building, but the damage is already done. Rather than acting as your fire department, the command center should operate as the fire inspector, smoke alarms, and sprinkler system, looking for conditions that may potentially lead to a fire and correcting those conditions, and if a fire does start, detecting it before it has a chance to spread and before anyone is affected by it.

The primary goal of the command center is to ensure customers are always able to do what the business promised, to ensure they can perform the tasks that generate income for the corporation. Bringing a computer system (server, mainframe, etc.) back up after it has crashed is too little, too late. When that happens the customers have been impacted and the command center is in reactive mode, hustling to restore service before customers give up and go elsewhere.

The successful command center is always proactive, there to monitor and resolve events at the earliest possible time to prevent a system outage. The environment is quiet, calm, and collected at all times. Potential problems are addressed and corrected before they can take down your systems.

Chapter One

What is an Operations Command and Control Center?

The command center is the lifeline of an organization. It is like the body's nervous system: constantly monitoring and sending alerts to the brain as events occur, with the brain issuing commands to other body functions to keep the body operating as it should. The command center enables an organization to function as designed, to perform day-to-day operations regardless of what is happening around it, in a manner in which no one realizes it is there but everyone knows who is in charge when there is trouble.

The command center monitors the environment and is ready to act quickly and decisively to a threat or potential threat to that environment. Everyone in and out of the command center who may at some point need to interact with it should know the roles and responsibilities of the command center or be able to easily find that information.

Each role and function that is performed by command center staff must have a fully documented set of procedures. Those procedures must be detailed yet simple enough to follow so that a new hire can perform all required functions with relative ease after an initial training period.

The command center is a place where order is maintained, especially if the world around it is falling apart. That is done by monitoring the environment and reacting to events, from the relatively harmless to a major crisis, using predefined procedures without deviation. Everything that happens in a command center must fall within its roles and responsibilities and must have a clearly defined procedure attached to it.

A command center provides leadership and guidance to ensure service and order is maintained. It should never be viewed as a mere information center or help/service desk. It is not a place where switchboard operators only help an organization's members maintain routine communications with each other. Nor is it a dumping ground for tasks and projects that no one else wants to do or other departments lack the personnel to perform. The command center staff members are not data entry clerks, and they should not be filling out daily checklists or updating a person's contact information.

There are many types of command centers. They include:

Data center management—oversees the central management and operating control for the computer systems that are the lifeline of most businesses, usually housed in data centers and large computer rooms.

Business application management—ensures applications that are critical to customers and businesses are always available and working as designed.

Civil management—oversees the central management and control of civil operational functions. Staff members in those centers monitor the metropolitan environment to ensure the safety of people and the proper operation of critical government services, adjusting services as required and ensuring proper constant movement.

Emergency (crisis) management—directs people, resources, and information, and controls events to avert a crisis/emergency and minimize/avoid impacts should an incident occur.

Types of command and control rooms and their responsibilities

- Command Center (CC)
  - > Data center and computer system
- Network Operation Centers (NOC)
  - > Network equipment and activity
- Tactical Operation Centers (TOC)
  - > Military operations
  - > Police and intelligence
- Security Operation Centers (SOC)
  - > Security agencies
  - > Government agencies
  - > Traffic management
  - > CCTV
- Emergency Operation Centers (EOC)
  - > Emergency services
- Combined Operation Centers (COS)
  - > Air traffic control
  - > Oil and gas
  - > Control rooms
  - > Broadcast
- Audio Visual (AV)
  - > Simulation and training
  - > Medical
- Social Media Command Center

Within each type of operations command center are several common functions. They include monitoring (which includes event management), incident management, coordinating and implementing applicable changes, and disaster recovery (also known as business continuity).

Goals

The overarching goal of a command center is to protect the integrity of its domain through proactive monitoring.

That means the command center staff is very busy making sure nothing outside of what is expected happens, that all systems are operating properly, and that customers and staff can perform what they need in a timely manner without any disruption of service.

Some days the staff will appear to be doing absolutely nothing; those are perfect days. Everyone is actually doing much more than it seems. They are watching, prepared to act should an alert appear on their monitors.

Other days the staff will be extremely busy, interacting with other staff members and support teams through headphones while being busy on their keyboards. When everyone is busy, they are reacting to alerts, performing initial diagnostics, and fixing the cause of an alert or notifying support and working with them to resolve the issue. They are also documenting everything that transpires.

Both scenarios would be considered a success if the environment worked flawlessly, where everything worked as it should; in other words, where customers and employees were able to function unhindered.

The next goal is to reduce the duration of any event that will negatively affect customers.

There will be times when an outage cannot be prevented, and the command center's main goal is breached. That is when the next goal kicks in: Reduce the duration of the impact. When the command center staff becomes aware of an outage, the incident management team takes over in order to coordinate service recovery efforts.

It's in this case that a command center with properly trained staff and effective incident management processes really shines. Watching the process as it unfolds is like watching poetry in motion. The environment remains calm; no one gets excited as the incident management team performs its critical functions. They establish conference calls to coordinate and collaborate with outside agencies and representatives to help restore service. They generate an incident trouble ticket (if not already created by automation), update the ticket, and send out notifications alerting the proper support teams, client managers, and senior management of the incident, all within a matter of minutes.

Next is ensuring that everything that should be monitored is monitored.

In any environment, there is always change. It is vital for the command center to know when something new has been added or something in the environment has been permanently or temporarily altered or removed. Anything new must be monitored from day one. Anything taken away needs to be removed from monitoring so that critical and highly paid support personnel do not spend countless hours and resources chasing ghosts.

The last goal is to ensure efficient use of resources.

A command center full of very busy people is not an ideal situation. Through the use of process optimization, automation, and standards, command center personnel resource requirements (the number of people required to fully operate) should be low — not too low to put the environment at risk but with enough staff to manage any situation.

Resource requirements need to take into account holidays, vacations, sick time, emergencies, and even a crisis (hurricanes, snow storms, and any other situation where the locality may declare a state of emergency). A properly executed and managed command center must be able to endure any situation with a set number of resources, including monitoring additional sites and businesses.

> In an efficient command center, the workload can double or triple without affecting service or the need for additional staff or resources. Basically, if the environment grows by 100%, the command center would be able to maintain current service levels without any increase in staff, overtime, or equipment.

How the goals are achieved

It is not enough for a command center to simply state a set of goals: Performance has to be tracked against those goals, if they are to be of any value to you and your clients.

In order for a command center to consistently meet its goals, they need to be fully documented and measurable.

That means establishing and enforcing standards for everything that takes place within the command center.

1. Establish standards

   Everyone must follow a detailed set of guidelines when implementing an application change, and when adding a new process, application, or business.

2. Enforcement of standards

   Any additional workload, whether it is moved from another location or is a new acquisition, must migrate to the current standards, policies, procedures, and practices. Any deviations or exceptions should be granted with a specific short-term time period and with a corresponding target date for achieving compliance. Exceptions granted without a deadline result in a moving target and the subsequent loss of standards and common processes.

3. Automated and accurate metrics

   Collecting and distributing the proper metrics for each goal provide guidance on the effectiveness of the command center. Trending metrics enables management to gauge and adjust resource and workload requirements.

4. Clear chain of command

   This is the place where the buck stops. Someone, not a low-level worker or a committee or group of co-managers but a specific senior-level manager, must be responsible and held accountable if something fails, whether it is a piece of equipment, a process, an application, or a function. The same applies if someone needs to escalate an issue. A clear chain of command should be documented so that whoever is unhappy with the current process or the way things are being handled has somewhere to go for resolution. That is also required to properly assign incidents that have been corrected but need a permanent resolution to prevent a recurrence.

To ensure consistency in meeting stated goals, all or most of these items need to be in place:

Automated alerting

Manually implementing monitoring for a new computer, application, or device; suppressing alerts for a scheduled event; or terminating monitoring when a system or application is removed from service is labor-intensive, time-consuming, and prone to errors. Automating those functions ensures that alerts are generated when they need to be and disabled when no longer required. Automation also ensures that those tasks are done when required, without delay.

Automated scheduling

The days of someone using a tracking sheet to process the daily workload are long gone. There are many simple-to-use tools that pay for themselves many times over simply by the number of human errors they eliminate.

Automated failure recovery

One of the reasons for extended batch processing delays or problems involving data is human error, usually during batch failure recovery efforts. Either because of unclear, incorrect, or missing restart instructions or a mistake in following the correct instructions, additional failures may occur, a database may get corrupted, data may get processed multiple times, or some data may not get processed at all. Preventing the failure from occurring in the first place in the best option, but that is not always possible. The next best option, where possible, is to automate the recovery process.

Support and management escalation procedures

When there is a problem, people are inclined to provide the person trying to fix it ample time in order to find and correct the cause of the issue. Before anyone realizes it, 5 minutes have turned into an hour. Escalation procedures, specifying timing requirements for each type of problem based on severity and impact, can prevent that from happening.

Independent problem management

Having a problem management team based outside of the command center and reporting to different management eliminates any conflict of interest in capturing and documenting problems. It provides an additional level of oversight so that required actions to identify and correct the cause of a problem are performed and a recurrence is prevented from happening.

Standards for hardware, software, and security (one consistent process for each function)

There are many benefits to implementing standards for hardware, software, and security. Though cost might be the main driver, standards promote efficiency and reduce errors by making it possible to automate many functions that would otherwise have to be performed manually. The lack of standards makes it difficult to implement enforceable procedures.

Change and Configuration Management Database (CCMDB)

Knowing what devices and applications a given change will affect is priceless information. A CCMDB helps to ensure that everyone affected by the change is made aware of it. That information is also invaluable when a failure occurs as a result of a change. Having a

CCMDB can mean the difference between a 2-hour outage and a 10-minute outage.

Known error database

When a problem occurs, identifying its cause usually takes the most time. Documenting each failure and the recovery actions in a known error database greatly reduces the recovery time for any subsequent failures or a similar type of failure that occurs elsewhere.

Failure management

When I first began working in Operations, long before command centers, efficiency, automation were around log sheets were used to track nightly processing. Like clockwork, every Friday night the same weekly batch job (a set of programs that performed a specific reconciliation function) failed. Tech support would get notified and 10 minutes later the batch job was back in the system, this time completing successfully. After that happened a third time, I took a walk over to the technical support staff member whose responsibility it was to correct the failure. I was curious why the job failed three weeks in a row. Roger explained that for about a year, the batch job was processing more data and needed additional storage space. So for the previous 12 months, Roger and the rest of the technical support staff would temporarily increase the amount of storage the batch process requested and then simply restart the job. That confused me even more. Why not simply make the fix permanent? "Job security" was Roger's response. The job was permanently fixed shortly after that exchange. Roger and the rest of the technical support team kept their jobs, but instead of fixing the same failures over and over again, they were able to devote time to identifying and correcting other bottlenecks and nuisances. The cause of a failure needs to be identified and corrected to prevent that same failure from occurring a second time.

Standardized metrics reporting (includes daily, weekly, and monthly target hits and misses)

Unless everything performed in a command center is tracked, measured, and reported, meeting goals will be potluck. The proper metrics would have identified the batch process that had been failing every week over the course of a year. Weekly and monthly trending reports help identify potential problem areas, any anomalies, and possible resource—human or machine—issues before they become a problem.

Automated daily exception reporting

Daily exception reports are where problems are identified and corrected before they can lead to major problems.

Automated monthly reporting

This is your opportunity to shine, to show the world how well the command center is performing.

Automated trouble report generation

Creating trouble tickets manually is very time-consuming and prone to errors: Tickets may not get created for every incident or failure, or may get assigned to the wrong group or department, extending the problem-resolution time. Failures that are not tracked and corrected with a properly documented trouble ticket are more likely to recur.

Continuous performance reviews

This just goes without saying. Progress and change never stops, so neither should your efforts to find opportunities for improvement.

Outcomes of a poorly managed command center:

Business outages as a result of the lack of monitoring or alerts not being acted upon.

> If a new production server that is not yet being monitored runs out of storage space, your customers will know about it before you do. If the monitoring consoles are flooded with false alerts, the chances are quite high that a valid critical alert will be missed, leading to system failure, and once again, your customers will know about the failure before you do.

Additional staff will be required to address the high number of non-actionable alerts.

> Manual event and alert management is very time-consuming and may lead to a high number of alerts on the monitoring consoles. That will give the mistaken impression that additional staff is required to manage the workload.

Loss of business due to customers who are fed up with inconsistent system availability.

Loss of business when frustrated customers go elsewhere to place orders.

Low morale and high turnover due to heavy workload.

Increased operational costs as business divisions create their own monitoring centers.

Regulatory fines for not meeting delivery requirements (system availability, account update, etc.).

Taking those steps may seem like a lot of work or may appear to threaten job security. Actually, the opposite is true. It takes much more work to correct failures than it does to prevent them. Implementing automation and efficient processes may or may not threaten job security, but continually missing goals and having unhappy clients definitely will lead to job losses, starting from the top down.

Chapter Two

Composition of the Command Center

In order for a command center to be as effective as possible, the functions, organizational structure, layout, and physical location must be properly defined, planned, and implemented. That ensures they are properly aligned with and will help achieve the intended goals.

Functions

Careful consideration needs to be given to the functions performed within the confines of the command center. Adding functions that do not support your stated goals will increase costs and complexity. Leaving out critical functions might save the command center money but may cost the company much more in lost customers and, eventually, revenue.

The functions determine the type of work to be performed in the command center, and direct managerial oversight becomes vital during a crisis. Any function moved into the command center that doesn't lead toward the defined goals will take needed resources from those goals. Similarly, functions that have a direct impact on achieving defined goals but are housed outside of the command center, where direct managerial oversight is not possible, will make it difficult to meet those goals.

Unfortunately, the criticality of housing the proper functions within a command center may not become apparent until after a major crisis has occurred. If that happens during your watch, hopefully when you find new employment you'll give a little more consideration to function placement.

Below are the recommended functions for housing in an infrastructure command center.

Primary command center functions:

- Monitoring
- Console operations
- Incident management
- Technical support

Secondary functions:

- Physical security oversight
- Off-hour emergency change control
- Support for ancillary organizations
- Project initiation and management for process improvements
- Business (disaster) recovery and coordination

Function One: Monitoring

Monitoring alerts is the most important function of a command center. It doesn't matter what the alerts are, where they are coming from, or how they are generated, delivered, or displayed. Actually all that matters greatly—to the department charged with managing alerts, usually the event management team, and is covered later in this book. What matters most to the monitoring staff and to the businesses they support is how the alerts are treated when they're received by the command center.

A location that does not perform monitoring but performs corrective actions only when users call with a problem is a call center or a help-desk. It is not a command center.

An alert is simply a notification that an event has occurred. An event is something that happens out of the ordinary that could lead to a service disruption to customers. Usually an alert is a warning that if an event, something out of the ordinary, is left unchecked, it may lead to the failure of an application or piece of hardware (computer, server, network, or storage device) or may affect the integrity of your data or system.

In a properly monitored environment, anything out of the ordinary or outside of certain thresholds should cause an alert to be generated. The type of event and how important or critical it is determines the type of alert, where it is sent, and whether anything should automatically happen.

The command center should have a team whose main function is to monitor. In a mission critical environment, the worst reaction is to reduce the size of the monitoring team because there have been no problems.

There are no problems because the monitoring team has been doing its job. It means they are preventing problems from happening. If the monitoring team is constantly busy, then you have a serious problem. It means the alerts are not properly configured or your applications and computer systems are very unstable. Either way, your customers will not be happy.

Monitoring is not just the responsibility of the team watching the screens but of everyone, regardless of their role or function. Making sure everyone knows it's a shared responsibility helps ensure the main goal of the command center—a safe and normally operating environment—is foremost on everyone's mind. What happens after an alert is detected by command center staff depends on who performs the other critical functions mentioned above.

The most common types of monitoring are:

- Infrastructure
- Application
- Business application monitoring
- Batch

Infrastructure monitoring

A business's infrastructure consists of the core components and applications that support its day-to-day operation and that are used throughout its divisions. In order for most businesses to operate efficiently, different divisions share common components, such as data centers, communications equipment, and mainframe computers. They may also share common applications, such as mail, firewall, security, and server support.

Disruptions within the organization's infrastructure can affect employees and customers alike. One of the command center's core functions is to monitor the infrastructure. By monitoring it as a whole, the command center can determine whether an issue is global in nature and can engage the proper support teams. For example, when there are outages that don't get fixed quickly, the command center notifies senior management within the affected divisions. That allows the businesses to notify customers of the problem before those customers begin calling in. It is better to inform them than it is to leave them in the dark or have them mistakenly try to diagnose their own equipment. Customers who find they are continually trying to fix problems on their own computer when trying to access your applications, that magically disappear, will eventually get frustrated and go elsewhere.

Application and business application monitoring

These types of monitoring are similar but have a few major differences.

Application monitoring is a high-level view of the application, usually performed by the global command center team. It examines the hardware, network, programs, error messages, and other items required for the application to properly function.

Business Application Monitoring, or BAM, looks at the internal workings within the applications. It examines details: Are transactions moving as they should? Are customers able to navigate within the application? Is response time acceptable? In larger organizations, BAM is performed by a separate team and is usually referred to as the business command center.

Batch monitoring

Most businesses perform housekeeping functions—reconciling business activities—during overnight hours. A scheduling team, usually located outside of the command center but reporting into the same management chain, performs the administrative scheduling function during business hours. During off-hours when the programs required to perform all overnight processing execute, the command center should monitor batch processing.

Batch monitoring notifies the proper support team if there is a failure. It also notifies the proper business managers if batch is behind schedule and is not expected to complete within the required timeframe, which would trigger inquiries from customers asking why an order was not processed or why their account is not up-to-date.

Ensuring that overnight processing failures are resolved in a timely manner and that processing completes on time is a function performed best by a command center. Performing those functions outside of a command center usually results in repeat failures, frequent delays, and missed deadlines. Recurring batch failures and late completions usually result in your customers taking their business to a company that is more reliable.

While monitoring batch should fall within the command center, correcting a batch failure is normally assigned to the technical support team. Batch technical support, fixing what breaks during batch processing, is a function that can fall inside or outside of the command center. A determining factor might be the size of the technical support team. If it's small enough and there's room within the command center, direct management oversight of that function is preferential.

Monitoring definitions

E2E (End to End) business level

- View of the overall health of the business segment regardless of the underlying platforms.

- This type of monitor encompasses all aspects of the business segment, starting from the hardware level up to and including the entry points presented to the customer.

- Alerts detected by this type of monitor are severity 1 or severity 2, where an actual business or customer impact is detected (or imminent).

Application level

- View of the health of the major business applications, encompassing all platforms and network connections supporting them.

- This type of monitor detects application level alerts, starting from the hardware level up to and including the entry points and initial screens that the customer is presented.

- Alerts detected by this type of monitor are severity 1 or severity 2, where an actual business or customer impact is detected (or imminent).

Platform level

- View of the base platforms supporting the different businesses.

- This type of monitor detects hardware or system software alerts, including system resources (memory, CPU utilization) and components (Dasd, Network connections and interfaces, tape drives), storage and system software (operating system, individual tasks, etc.).

- Alerts detected by this type of monitor are severity 1, severity 2, severity 3, and severity 4, including threshold violations where no impact exists but is imminent if not corrected.

Infrastructure level

- View of the systems, components, and applications supporting the different data centers and businesses.

- This type of monitor detects hardware or system software alerts, including system and network resources (memory, CPU utilization) and components (storage, network connections and interfaces, media drives), and system software (operating system, database, individual tasks, etc.).

- Alerts detected by this type of monitor are severity 1, severity 2, severity 3, and severity 4, including threshold violations where no impact exists but is imminent if not corrected.

- Examples of the infrastructure monitored:
  - > Firewalls, routers, switches, BigIP, 3DNS, Tivoli servers, SAN, databases.

Function Two: Console Operations

Manual console operations using tracking and run sheets is a function from a bygone era. With the wide array of automation tools available on the market, or which can easily be developed in-house, no one should be entering commands on a system console or through an application that provides remote access to an operator console, except in emergency situations. For day-to-day operations, automation should perform all console-related functions. If you manage a command center where tracking sheets are still in use, it might be a good idea to update your resume.

Within a command center, the same team usually performs both the monitoring and the console operations functions. In the old days operators were busy from the time they sat down at the start of their shift until they left at the end of their shift, typing commands on the system console in response to various alerts and messages.

It is an unsustainable model because it requires additional staff whenever the workload increases. That practice increases the number and duration of outages because operators who are busy entering commands are more likely to miss critical alerts. Doubling the workload means you would need twice as many staff members, and operators who are busy entering commands will be delayed in reacting to critical alerts. That will result in outages when the condition causing the alert is not resolved in time.

The goal for console operations, either within a command center or stand-alone, should be ZERO manual intervention.

That means no one should have to touch the system console except in very rare situations, such as invoking and confirming disaster recovery actions. With today's suite of automation tools, manual intervention is no longer required, nor can it be justified, and should be eliminated if it is done in your command center.

Items to automate or eliminate

There are many manual processes that can and should be automated. Among them are:

Start of day or end of day actions

These should be performed by the scheduling application or system automation. Many delays to start of day are caused by a breakdown in communication. An e-mail or a phone call from the application administrators—meant to inform operations to begin overnight processing or to make the application available for start of day—will be missed, especially if the intended recipient is unavailable. The breakdown will eventually be caught, but by then there will be some form of impact to the business, such as transactions that did not get processed or customers trying to access an application that isn't available.

Messages waiting for a response

Eliminating these reduces the chance for missed critical messages. Many system type software applications produce their own warning message in order to protect you, the customer. Some may warn not to begin application x until y is available. Others may ask for a new device after several write or read errors. Before automation tools were available, a common practice among business application developers as a way of implementing safeguards was to issue a message asking for an operator to respond "Y" at the appropriate time, such as when files have been closed or opened, or a needed file has been received.

Having someone look for and respond to those types of messages is simply asking for trouble. For one, hidden between the messages might be a warning of a critical system error. Missed critical system error messages will usually lead to a system failure, affecting an untold number of customers. Secondly, hours can be lost by an application that is waiting for an operator to respond "Y" for a business transaction file that was already received. By the time someone responds "Y," the window for processing that file may have expired, or the results from that application will not be ready in time for a handoff to the next system. Delays in taking action for critical events can be reduced or eliminated by stopping those messages at the source and automating the required actions.

Started task/online failure recovery

Instituting automated failure recovery ensures outages and impacts are kept to a minimum. When a system or business application fails, the normal response is to attempt a restart as quickly as possible so that the impact is kept to a minimum. In most cases, that is enough to restore service, followed by root cause analysis to find and correct the cause of the failure. Sometimes, due to internal application cleanup routines, two restarts are required. When performed manually, that can take anywhere from a few minutes to hours, depending on when each failure is noticed. Additional delays occur if an operator doesn't know the proper startup command or issues the wrong command, such as the start of day rather than a recovery startup command, causing data integrity issues which then take hours and an untold number of development and support staff members to correct.

Once console functions are automated, analysts (going forward analyst would be a more appropriate title rather than operator) are free to perform more critical functions, such as monitoring the alert screens, resolving open incidents, or looking for process improvement opportunities.

Function Three: Incident Management

Incident management is one of the terms given to the process of resolving an issue immediately after it has occurred, in order to avoid or reduce any impact caused by the event. It is the process of coordinating the recovery of a failure where a business impact is in progress or imminent if not resolved quickly. That includes ensuring that a trouble ticket is created, logging all activities that are performed as part of the recovery effort, engaging the proper support teams, and notifying management at prescribed intervals. All of those actions are usually required to be done in an expedited, time-sensitive manner.

When the monitoring team gets an alert for an anomaly that affects the proper operation of a function or application, it is handed over to the incident management team. Those types of issues are classified as incidents.

An incident is something that occurs and disrupts the norm, such as a power failure to a data center, a computer or application that stops working, or a hardware failure that affects the proper operation of anything used by your customers. If it affects a certain number of internal employees, external customers, or the proper operation of a key function, or if it has a large financial impact, then the incident becomes a high severity incident. The high severity incident would be upgraded to a crisis if the affected functions pose a risk to the integrity of your business. In other words, if you are at risk of losing credibility with your customers or making the newspaper headlines in a negative manner. (In a crisis situation, the corporate CIO and CEO are usually notified to ensure they are aware of the situation should senior-level customers or the press begin calling about it.)

The recommendation is to perform incident management from within the command center.

To understand why, you need to consider the purpose of the incident management team and how critical it is to the goals of the command center.

> If the main goal of the command center is to eliminate or reduce impacts to the businesses it serves, then command center management needs to make sure the incident management team is working diligently to resolve any outstanding incidents. That is much easier to accomplish when they are in the same room and report to the same management.

Managing an incident when the team driving the resolution process does not report to you is extremely difficult.

1. The incident management team not only needs to be in the same room but it also must report to the command center director.
2. The command center director is ultimately responsible for ensuring goals are met and problems are resolved in a timely manner.
3. When too many incidents occur or their durations begin to get longer, it is the command center director who is usually held accountable.

If you are going to be held accountable, wouldn't you want to own the entire resolution process?

Are you comfortable taking responsibility for something beyond your control?

The major roles and responsibilities of the incident management team include the following:

- Manage all severity 1 and severity 2 incidents through resolution.
- Notify management and technical support of incidents.
- Create and update incident trouble tickets.
- Open and lead conference bridge.
- Engage all support and emergency response groups as required.
- Resolve incident trouble tickets.

Function Four: Technical Support

It is always in the best interests of the business and the command center to resolve an issue as quickly as possible. In order for that to happen, the command center monitoring staff must be able to properly diagnose each alert in order to take the proper corrective actions or to notify the appropriate technical help.

Certain types of failures can be identified and corrected by senior analysts within the command center without the need for additional support. That is especially true with batch processing type failures, such as those caused by read/write or space errors. Valuable time is saved by performing the function within the command center, but it comes at a price: Occasionally mistakes will be made that will lead to a major customer-visible incident. With the proper controls the risks can be mitigated, but that is a decision the command center director needs to make: Should the command center staff perform level-one technical support?

For performing level-one support, there are two trains of thought.

One is that initial diagnosis and resolution should be performed within the command center. In other words, the staff in the command center should perform the functions of level-one support: Identify what caused the alert or incident and attempt to resolve it. If greater expertise is required, they would contact the appropriate level-two (system or application) technical support team.

The second train of thought is for the staff in the command center to perform the initial diagnosis, then contact the appropriate level-one or level-two support team to fix the issue.

Each approach has pros and cons, so it is up to the operations director and the amount of support provided from above. Performing initial diagnostics to determine the cause of a problem saves time by pinpointing the correct support team to call. That should be done regardless of which train of thought is followed. Calling the wrong support team will delay resolution of the event, thereby increasing the chances for it to become an incident that may affect your clients.

Attempting to fix the issue and close the alert is a different matter altogether. Having someone in the command center fix it, basically performing level-one technical support, does have many benefits but carries some risks as well.

Here are the pros and cons for each train of thought.

Command center technical support performing initial diagnosis only

Pros:

Reduces risk of making a mistake

The person who owns the application where the failure occurred will be more knowledgeable with the internal workings and recovery steps of the application and less likely to make a mistake when repairing the cause of the failure.

Reduces repeat occurrences

The person responsible would try to make a permanent repair to avoid similar situations in the future and to prevent the event from happening elsewhere. Preventing the event from happening ensures the person will not be disturbed while sleeping or otherwise engaged in a social activity.

Cons:

Longer resolution time

Resolution of the problem and restoration of service or batch processing is delayed while the staff investigates who owns the event, contacts that person, then waits for the person to get online to investigate and correct the issue.

Loss of technical skills

Command center staff will begin to lose any technical skills they have and may not learn new ones.

Command center technical support performing initial diagnosis and level-one support (fixing the event)

Pros:

Reduces resolution time

There's no need to track down support and wait while they sign on and investigate the incident.

Improves technical skills

The staff's skills improve, and they can lend more support to technical teams.

Cons:

Increases chance for mistakes

The probability of making a critical mistake that would affect customers increases, especially for items that are not properly documented.

Increase in repeat failures

There's no motivation for staff to permanently correct repeat failures because of the mistaken fear that it may lead to a reduction of the number of required technical staff members.

Mistakes made by developers and users continue

Because the fixes are made by command center staff, the teams who own the application may not be aware of the issue and are more likely to keep repeating the same mistakes.

Another consideration that may help determine where technical support functions are performed is the size of the technical support team. Shops with a large level-one technical support team may not have the required amount of space in the command center to house everyone. But then again, a shop with a very large level-one technical support team has other problems to worry about: Why are there enough failures to warrant a large technical support team?

Secondary Functions

Secondary functions can be performed inside or outside of the command center, depending on the location of the command center and its budgeting requirements. Those functions include oversight of data center access, business/disaster recovery and coordination, and project initiation and management for process improvement.

Data center access oversight

Most command centers are 24/7 sites, so at times it is economical for command center staff to provide screening services for anyone requiring access to the data center. It is even beneficial, especially during off-hours, for the command center to monitor and control who goes in and out of a data center because it's also responsible for monitoring the equipment in the data center. In most cases, the people who need access to the data center during off-hours are support personnel who've been called in by the command center.

Business (disaster) recovery and coordination

In most instances, especially with data center and mainframe computer issues, the command center staff performs the disaster recovery coordination. The business recovery or data center directors make the decision to initiate the disaster recovery steps, but the command center staff executes the initial recovery steps, makes all required notifications, and engages all support staff as needed.

Project initiation and management for process improvements

The project initiation function helps ensure the command center does not suddenly get work no one was expecting. Providing team members on key projects ensures all command center needs and requirements are considered and, hopefully, met.

Process improvement helps the command center continually improve and makes recommendations to application teams that are having problems meeting deadlines. The team provides recommendations to the standards committees based on lessons learned and detailed analysis of monitoring and incident management.

- It is preferable to have that function performed within the command center, but it could be just as easily done from the outside but in close proximity. The team performing the function should visit the command center in order to learn where the problems are and what requires the most attention.

The operational and organizational muscle of the command center leadership determines where some of those functions are performed. Some functions by nature belong within the command center without question, such as monitoring. The location for other functions is determined by the goals of the command center. Where those functions fall may ultimately depend on which department leader has more sway with senior management.

When the functions within the command center are determined, you can then start building the organizational structure. That will comprise the people doing the day-to-day work, supervisors, managers, and anyone else required to ensure the proper operation of the center.

Once the organizational structure is determined, the next step is to begin designing the command center.

Chapter Three

Organizational Structure

After the command center's functions are determined, the next step is to define its roles and responsibilities. Taken as a whole, those roles and responsibilities should be a combination of the following, depending on the type of command center.

Roles and responsibilities

Command center management

These are the roles and responsibilities for every manager within the command center.

- Achieve stated goals.

  Once a decision is made on what the command center goals will be, it is each manager's responsibility to ensure the overall goals and the ones related to their specific function and team are met.

- Monitor, manage, and control the environment. Monitor and react to alerts by managing and performing recovery actions for systems and their associated hardware, application and system software, and batch scheduling within the command center's domain.

  It is the manager's responsibility to ensure alerts are addressed in a timely manner. The manager accepts blame for every outage caused because an alert was missed or improperly handled or there were excessive delays in notifying the proper support teams. The manager is also responsible for following up with the proper teams in order to correct a monitoring deficiency for an application or system that suffers an outage that could have been prevented if the command center had received an alert. A preventable outage to an unmonitored application or computer system should only happen once.

- Ensure all service level agreements (SLAs) or quality indicators (QIs) are met to provide consistent service to the user community.

That is basically a way to measure how well the command center is able to meet its obligations to its customers.

For example, if command center management has agreed to have a store's pricing and inventory system updated and available by 8:00 a.m. each morning, then anytime the system is not updated and available at 8:00 a.m. would count as missing a key deliverable. (It is irrelevant if the store doesn't open till 9:00 a.m. and the systems are updated and available before then; it is still counted as a missed deliverable once the 8:00 a.m. SLA is missed.)

A mistake that some command center managers make is to count a missed deliverable only if someone calls to complain. That is a very dangerous path to take because the metrics become discretionary and subjective rather than based on objective events and measurements.

- Work with business services to ensure current SLAs or QIs are correctly structured in order to provide maximum recovery windows without jeopardizing service to the user community.

Normally, a requirement when signing an SLA or QI agreement is that each deliverable has a sufficient recovery window such that even with failures during processing, the target deadline can still be met. There will be times where a business application or a system change may adversely affect a deliverable by completely eliminating the recovery window and causing the target deadline to be missed on a regular basis. Managers need to be cognizant of those events in order to take corrective actions, either by negotiating a new target deadline or correcting the condition that eliminated the recovery window.

- Provide real-time escalation, recovery, and restore capabilities for any failure of service; notify the proper support teams; and coordinate recovery as needed.

  The manager is responsible for ensuring the incident management procedures are properly followed and invoked in a timely manner. In situations where the incident management team is housed outside of the command center, the manager is still responsible for ensuring the team is engaged as soon as possible for every incident and the proper actions are taken as required. That is one of the reasons it is best to place the incident management team inside the command center.

- Coordinate or execute the proper shutdown and load for systems as required for approved changes (following change control standard procedures).

  There are many types of changes where the operational team within the command center will be required to implement, assist with, or coordinate activities between teams. The managers are responsible to ensure those changes are reviewed for approval or rejection in a timely manner and to coordinate the appropriate actions for all fully approved change requests.

- Escalate all major issues and notify senior management— whether they're in operations or the affected businesses— ensuring the right people know of the incident at the right time.

- Constantly review existing processes and research new ones for possible automation improvements or enhancements, designing and installing special project improvements or enhancements whenever necessary.

  In a command center environment, automation is a must, especially when a percentage of client-impacting outages are caused by human error. The managers need to be the main drivers for automation and to make sure everyone is aware that automating a task will not eliminate jobs but rather will allow staff to focus on their core function. A manager who does not believe in and promote automation has no business being in a command center.

- Comply with audit and security rules and regulations, and ensure established command center procedures are properly documented, updated, and followed.

- Ensure command center disaster recovery procedures are in place and tested to ensure they meet requirements, and provide support and coordination services for business or data center disaster recovery testing or live events.

  That includes disaster recovery planning and testing for data center equipment, as well as the actual functions of the command center itself.

- Provide technical support, advice, process improvement recommendations, and implementation assistance to application teams on major projects and changes.

As the focal point, the command center is in a position to observe and gather best practices from projects and changes performed by the various groups it interacts with. Identifying best practices and changes that may have an adverse affect on an application or SLAs and disseminating that information to all groups allows the managers to keep recovery windows as large as possible, helping keep or exceed service level targets.

- Provide daily management status reports and metrics, reviewing them daily for trends and potential problems.

  That is where potential problems are identified and addressed before they have a negative impact on the command center or the businesses supported. Unless the managers know what happens daily and the current trends, they will not be in a position to prevent problems but instead will be busy explaining why certain issues weren't identified and addressed.

- Perform human resources duties as needed to ensure the required number of staff members are on duty and to provide initial and refresher training as needed.

Monitoring and operational staff

- Monitor alerting screens and resolve all issues that do not impact any clients (usually classified as severity 3 or higher). Notify support teams as required.

  That is their core responsibility, and anything that interferes with the function needs to be brought to management's attention as soon as possible. Requests to ignore alerts should be rejected and escalated to management if the support team refuses to address and prevent non-actionable alerts from being displayed on the monitoring screens.

- Engage the incident management team for all issues that impact clients (usually classified as severity 1 and 2).

- Ensure a trouble ticket exists for each issue and update it as required.

- Ensure the proper operation of managed platforms and systems, applications operating on managed platforms, and infrastructure supporting platforms and applications.

  That goes hand in hand with monitoring. Any platform, system, and application managed by the team should have the appropriate level of monitoring enabled so that alerts are sent to the monitoring screens as required.

- Support incident, change, and problem management teams as required.

- Monitor batch processing.

- Perform operational and oversight responsibilities as required to ensure all SLAs are met.

- Notify management of any potential breach of an SLA.

- Perform disaster recovery functions as required.

- Escalate any event or team that interferes with the ability to perform required duties to management.

Incident management

The incident management team members' roles and responsibilities:

- Manage all severity 1 and severity 2 incidents through their resolution.

- Properly classify, categorize, and record all incidents.

- Update and review the known-error database for a previous matching error and its solution.

- Notify management and technical support when necessary.

- Create (if not already done so by automation or the unit reporting the incident) and update incident trouble tickets.

- Open and lead incident resolution conference bridge line.

- Engage all support and emergency response groups as required.

- Resolve incident trouble tickets.

- Produce daily, weekly, and monthly management reports.

- Measure deliverables against business objectives and make recommendations for improvements. Ensure service-level objectives for incident resolution, support notification, and management escalations and notifications are met.

- Regularly review and update incident management processes and procedures.

- Ensure one consistent incident management process is implemented and followed throughout the organization.

Technical support

Command center technical support team members' roles and responsibilities:

- Ensure all batch processing SLAs are met.

- Review, analyze, and correct batch processing failures and other issues as required to ensure processing is completed to standards.

- Notify application support as required for batch restart recovery.

- Ensure a fully documented trouble ticket exists for each failure. (The trouble ticket should be created and assigned to the proper team by automation.)

- Ensure an emergency change record exists for any changes to batch that affect how confidential data is created, changed, stored, or read.

- Initiate and support automation projects to eliminate manual setups and interventions, ensuring automatic scheduling of production and on-request batch processes.

- Support and implement emergency change control requests for batch failure recovery.

- Produce daily, weekly, and monthly management reports.

- Continually perform process improvement assessments and provide recommendations to application teams.

- Analyze command center processes for improvements.

- Implement process improvements using standard change management procedures.

- Regularly review and update technical support processes and procedures.

- Ensure one consistent technical support process is implemented and followed throughout the command center.

Chapter Four

Command Center Design

There are many considerations that go into the design and build of a command center. Budget is one of the most important concerns. Go too high and sticker shock will derail your project: You'll end up performing minor upgrades to your existing space. Go too low and you may not have the resources you need to meet your goals. There is a middle ground, and the difficulty lies in finding the proper balance between must have, need to have, like to have, and "wow" factor.

In case you think otherwise, there is value in some wow factor: It is a great marketing tool and is usually backed up with strong incident-prevention results. The trick is not to go overboard. The purpose of wow factor is to show clients how far you are willing to go in order to safeguard their business and clients, not to impress your staff or management. An over-the-top video conference room with lifelike holographic 3D images of the person on the other end will not impress clients. A video wall showing green next to each of their businesses will.

If your event management team can fit all incoming alerts onto one monitoring screen, then there is no need for a video wall. If you can get eyes on all monitoring screens without the need to switch between views, then there is no need for a video wall. The intent is to have many eyes on the monitoring screens at all times. Unless your command center monitors only a few businesses or applications, that is very difficult to do without a video wall.

The video wall gives a small number of people the ability to properly monitor a large environment. In one glance a video wall can tell management and anyone else entering the command center the health of the businesses supported.

Another consideration is the size of the environment being monitored: the number of data centers, computer systems, branches, business applications, etc., to be monitored. Those numbers, in conjunction with the organizational structure, will provide the staffing and video wall requirements, which in turn determine the minimum space requirements for your command center.

Consideration needs to be given to a hot backup, dividing the workload among two or more command centers that can take on the workload should one fail, or recovery at an alternate location within a specific timeframe without impact to the controlled environment. The main factors when deciding which option to implement are budget and the impact of any lost time in performing command center functions. If the command center must be available at all times no matter what, then the best option is to divide the workload across multiple locations that back up each other.

During the design stage, the following should be addressed: the footprint, the physical location, and other design considerations.

The footprint takes into account whether to build, buy, lease, or use existing space for the command center. The main drivers for the footprint are functions to be performed, number of seats required, growth expectations (organic or through acquisition), and disaster recovery requirements. Of course, budget will be a main concern, that is, unless you've already proven the value of a properly built and managed command center.

The physical location of the command center should be different from where the equipment or environment that's under control is located so that an event that disables the data center will not also disable the command center. The location needs to be accessible during a crisis, meaning that staff should be able to get to and leave from the location or have available lodging nearby during an emergency situation when travel restrictions are imposed.

Other considerations for location include the command center's ability to operate during a crisis where there are power and communication disruptions and the ability to invoke data center or command center disaster recovery procedures when required.

At this stage it's best to engage an audio/video integration firm and an architect who are experienced with command center designs.

Security
Due to the critical nature of the functions performed, the sensitive nature of the information, and the level of authority of active system consoles, a command center is usually a highly restricted area. In some cases access will need to be controlled by an entry portal where each person must prove authorization before being granted access. In locations that require a secured entry portal, there must be the ability to prevent tailgating, where multiple persons are able to gain access using one authorization or access card. Cameras should also record who enters and exists.

Comfort and environmental considerations
The command center should be designed to operate as efficiently as possible while providing a comfortable environment for staff that needs to be alert for long periods of time. Implementing a video wall helps reduce the amount of space and staff required, but it needs to be designed so that it doesn't cause undo strain on the staff using it. The environment must also limit how noise travels so that two people sitting next to each other can see the video wall yet can have separate phone conversations.

Design considerations

There are numerous design considerations for a command center, including that it be geographically friendly and that a large staff can operate comfortably in a small open environment without impacting each other's work efforts. Space requirements need to be determined, as well as the location, layout, size, and number of video screens for the video wall. In addition, there are considerations for employees (such as the duration of their shifts, lighting, airflow, sounds, and comfort).

The command center should be self-contained with an uninterruptible power supply, a combination of batteries and generators so that power is never lost to critical and sensitive computer equipment.

Everything within the command center space should include onsite and offsite redundancy for application and data servers. It should have redundant network equipment and connections as well as redundant voice communication.

It is also a good idea to include a war room, which is a location where management can gather during a crisis without impacting the ongoing incident and crisis management team and conference calls.

Chapter Five

Command Center Interactions

Monitoring and incident, change, and problem management are very tightly intertwined and must work closely together to ensure issues are prevented or corrected as quickly as possible, and that they do not recur.

Monitoring process

Monitoring should be proactive, not reactive. Its purpose is to sound an alert when something has the potential for failing, not to notify when something breaks. It alerts the right people that a failure may occur if an action is not taken to correct the event that just occurred.

Early warning alerting and monitoring can be done in various ways and through numerous tools. One way is by setting thresholds so that alerts are generated when an event reaches a specified value. For example, an alert would be generated if the hard drive on a server with 500 MB of space gets down to 75 MB free, in other words if 85% of the available space is used. The first alert would be sent to the command center (and hopefully the support staff) when available space on the drive reaches 15%. When the first alert shows up, someone should be dispatched to investigate and correct the issue. If the incident is not corrected, a second alert would be generated and sent when available space reaches 10%. A third alert would be sent when the available space reaches 5%. If the condition is not fixed, when the available space reaches zero, the server will crash and your customers will be unable to perform the functions that generate your income. If you let that happen often enough, your customers will take their business elsewhere.

Some support team members will want to know when available space reaches, let's say 15%, but will not act until it reaches 10%. They will instruct the command center member calling them to ignore the alert and to call back when available space reaches 10%. That is a mistake, and any request to ignore an alert should be rejected. Situations like that can be addressed by sending the 15% alert only to the support team and the subsequent alerts to the command center. Ignoring alerts on the command center monitoring screens for any reason is a recipe for disaster. Before long, the monitoring screens will be flooded with non-actionable alerts, increasing the likelihood for a real alert to be missed and an outage to occur.

Available space on a hard drive is one example, but the monitoring team will receive hundreds of types of alerts. Everything that might affect the integrity of the domain for which the command center is responsible must have a way to send a notification if a potential failure may occur, before the situation becomes critical.

Another way for generating early warning detection alerts is through applications internal error reporting routines, picking up critical messages and displaying them on the monitoring screens. Those types of alerts are implemented with the aid of the application development team.

Incident management process

An incident management team with a properly defined and executed process helps to ensure problems are well-documented, broadcast to all required parties, and resolved as quickly as possible. One of the most important functions of the incident management team is to document every action taken during the incident management process. Who is called, who responds, who does what, and what happens during the process must all be documented in the trouble ticket that's created for each specific event.

Never, ever combine the incident management and problem management processes within a single team. It is a major conflict of interest and a recipe for disaster! In fact, the problem management function should not fall within the command center but should be an autonomous team reporting to a senior level in order to prevent any conflict of interest between it and the groups with which it interacts.

In addition to managing the incident resolution process, the incident management team also performs monitoring, usually at a high level that allows them to correlate global-type impacts to a specific event or problem, helping to prevent global issues or to reduce outage duration.

Change management process

Command centers by their nature are heavily involved in the change management process. That happens for two reasons. First, in many cases the change control teams operate only during business hours, so the command center management assumes some of the oversight function during emergencies in order to resolve an ongoing incident that affects users. Second, many of the changes will be performed on systems they manage, and as a result they're an interested party in the success or failure of those changes. In some cases, command center staff involvement is required in order to implement certain changes.

It is in the best interests of the command center to develop a healthy relationship with the change management teams. There are many instances where the watchful eyes of an alert change management staff member catch pending changes that may negatively impact a managed system. Another benefit of a maintaining a healthy relationship is that the change management teams can help implement and enforce standards defined by the command centers through process improvement initiatives.

Problem management process

A well-implemented problem management process helps to ensure problems have a permanent solution and actions have been taken to prevent the problem in the future or to resolve it quicker if there is a recurrence.

As part of the problem management process, tasks may get assigned to the event management team to implement monitoring or correct alerting for problems that could have been prevented if the proper monitoring was in place.

Tools and procedures should also be in place for all problems and corrective actions to be documented and available for the incident management team to utilize in order to reduce outage durations for known errors.

A good practice is to use ITIL recommendations as a basis to build on for each of those processes.

> ITIL (IT Infrastructure Library) is a framework of best practices for the five core processes used by information technology to identify, plan, deliver, and support IT services. The five core processes are service strategy, service design, service transition, service operation, and continual service improvement. Additional information can be found on the ITIL website: http://www.itil-officialsite.com

Do's and Don'ts

Do have well-documented procedures for the command center's role in monitoring, change management, disaster recovery, escalation, incident management, security management, event management, and problem management. Those procedures must be followed by everyone. There should be no exceptions, unless specifically accounted for in the procedures.

Do have well-documented guidelines for the different severity levels. They will determine how each outage is treated, the types and frequency of notifications, and the escalation points. Ambiguous definitions may result in insufficient notifications and escalations leading to extended delays in resolving a major problem. Frequent reviews should be performed to make sure the guidelines are properly implemented.

Do centralize all of your monitoring. All systems and applications that are critical to the operation of the businesses and divisions supported should be monitored centrally by the command center. That allows the command center to quickly determine whether a problem is global in nature and speeds up the recovery process. Knowing which alerts are outstanding when a major problem occurs helps to identify the proper support teams to engage and reduces the length of the problem.

Do standardize your monitoring tools and create best practices profiles so that certain functions can be fully automated, such as the addition of monitoring on a new production server.

Do act on every alert. Every alert that the command center receives should be acted upon. If a support staff member says to ignore an alert for whatever reason, the response should always be no. The alert should be documented with a corresponding trouble ticket. That should be a onetime-only alert. The support teams must correct the alerting system so that the alert is triggered only when there is an actionable issue.

Don't allow individual teams to utilize stand-alone products if there is a standard monitoring tool defined for a given platform.

Don't allow manual checks of an applications function. Relying on someone to manually check application functionality causes delays and has the potential for extended outages. Operators should be automatically alerted when an exception occurs that may impact application functionality.

Don't let support teams perform their own monitoring exclusively. Some teams may want to perform their own monitoring; that is not acceptable. It is OK if they want a view of what the command center sees. It is not OK to let them perform monitoring instead of the command center. Departments and teams that perform their own monitoring with no oversight tend to hide their dirty laundry. They also tend to apply temporary fixes. As a result, you will have more outages, longer outage times, and a higher percentage of recurring outages. Because there's no oversight, senior management is usually unaware of the number or scope of the outages. Customers usually take their business elsewhere and senior management is left wondering why they did so.

When the command center performs the monitoring, it serves two purposes.

First, the command center is able to quickly determine whether a problem in one area is affecting other areas. If a communications line goes down and several businesses suddenly go red, command center staff will know which support teams to notify first. A team monitoring its own area may not be aware of the communications failure and will spend valuable time diagnosing the problem.

The second purpose is transparency. Teams that are being watched by others tend to run better, with fewer problems. When something breaks, they tend to find a permanent solution so that the same issue doesn't recur.

Don't ignore alerts. Ignoring alerts is a sure way of getting into trouble. At some point a mistake will be made and someone will ignore the wrong alert. Avoid the problem altogether by making sure non-actionable alerts are not even seen.

Don't let the monitoring screens get flooded with alerts. A monitoring screen that's flooded with alerts makes it very easy to miss a critical alert. Alerts need to be acted upon and corrected as soon as possible. It is not acceptable to let alerts sit in the queue until the support teams' regular work hours. If the condition is acceptable during off-hours, then the alert should only be generated when it is not acceptable and when someone is available to work on the problem. Alerts that don't get addressed within a specific timeframe should get escalated to the next level of management.

Chapter Six

Automation

A command center that is able to monitor and control an organization's primary information systems and associated data centers and applications is in an ideal position to provide additional value to its clients.

Being in the center of those activities means that the command center has the ability to influence and impact almost everything. Global problems get brought to the command center's attention. Application delays and outages, overnight processing delays, change-related issues, and many other global-type problems make their way to the command center. Therefore, when performing incident management, the command center gets a glimpse into the inner workings of every business, application, and team with which it interacts.

From that perspective, the command center staff has a duty to keep a watchful eye out for opportunities to eliminate and reduce wasteful practices and to initiate process improvements.

When looking for opportunities to improve service, there should be no boundaries. Anything that falls within the scope of the command center would fall under the command center management's responsibility to improve. Anything that falls outside of its scope of authority would be assigned to the management for the responsible party.

One of the best ways to improve service is through the use of automation. Through automation, delays and errors caused by human interaction can be reduced or eliminated. If you're unsure how useful automation can be in your environment, look through your outage logs. How many times has an application been delayed because an outstanding message waiting for a response went unnoticed for hours? How many incidents, such as double postings of orders or transactions, were caused by a procedural error or technical support oversight? Most of those incidents can be eliminated or minimized with the use of automation.

Automation can be applied to just about any task performed by a human being that does not require thought and analysis. Any repeatable process that follows a specific pattern can be automated. It is the command center's responsibility to its clients to point out the potential benefits of automation any time it encounters an inefficient or error-prone manual process, regardless of who is performing the task.

There are many tools that allow a command center to automate just about anything. If an existing tool doesn't perform the automation you need, it is simple enough to build your own. In this day and age, there is absolutely no reason for someone to manually perform a repeatable task on a regular basis.

Automation allows the command center staff to concentrate on monitoring rather than performing manual tasks. It enables the command center to operate better with less people.

Equally important, automation enables the command center to take on additional workload without the need for additional staff, space, or equipment.

An automation strategy should encompass each of the following:

- Automated alerting and escalation
- Automated systems management and console operations (meaning zero manual intervention)
- Automated batch job scheduling/setup/recovery
- Automated trouble ticket and report generation
- Automated help-desk: self-service
- Automated daily exception reporting

Automated alerting and escalation

The purpose of automated alerting and escalation is to ensure every production system is monitored, that only production alerts get sent to the command center monitoring screens and to ensure alerts are resolved in a timely manner.

Here are a few examples where automation can be effectively applied.

1. One of the most common tasks performed by command center staff is watching alerts and notifying the proper support staff. Any delays in either of those could result in a customer impact or a longer impact, if unavoidable. Technology is also available to automatically notify the proper on-call person via cell, home phone, or e-mail, and to continue going up the chain of command until someone is reached. The alerting system would also notify support team managers and the command center if support is not responding.

Automating calls to the on-call support person via his or her preferred method, such as a cell or home phone, for a given alert can save valuable time and reduce the likelihood of notifying the wrong person. Coupled with automated escalation to the backup support person and then to the department manager will mean the difference between preventing an outage or an extended outage.

A common mistake to avoid once support acknowledges an alert notification is to wait indefinitely for the cause of the alert to be addressed. Some support staff members lose track of time when trying to correct a difficult issue, with minutes turning into hours without any signs of progress. To prevent that from happening, the support person working on the issue should be asked for a status update at regular intervals, say, every 30 minutes. After x number of intervals, depending on the severity and criticality of the alert, notification would then go to the support team manager. Automating the status update request and the management escalation will prevent support, as well as the command center staff, from losing track of time.

Once those functions are automated, a noticeable reduction should be seen in the outage duration metrics.

2. The days of an operator manually going through a checklist to validate that everything is working as it should be are long gone. Technology now exists that can automatically validate that an application is working properly, that all prerequisites and components are available, and that can detect potential problems and then notify the command center and appropriate support teams with an alert detailing the problem found.

Have you ever been frustrated when the check engine light in your car comes on when you know full well that it was a specific sensor that raised the red flag? An automated checklist is similar to your car's numerous sensors, constantly checking every component. One important difference is that when automation detects a problem, rather than telling you to check the application, it will tell you specifically which sensor detected the problem and the conditions that were encountered.

3. As part of an automated solution, synchronizing alerts with the change and inventory management systems will prevent non-actionable alerts caused during the implementation of an approved change, and can help ensure all production systems have proper alerting.

All IT departments should require every production system to be monitored. If your environment doesn't have that requirement, then perhaps a review of your IT standards might be a good starting point. Integrating your monitoring application with the inventory system makes it possible for every new production system to generate alerts from day one, without the need for anyone to make a request for monitoring or to implement new monitoring. The opposite would occur for decommissioned systems: Monitoring is automatically disabled, eliminating the need for a formal request or for someone to manually disable it.

Automated systems management and console operations

The purpose of automating systems management and console operations is to ensure zero manual processing for all business-as-usual tasks, allowing command center staff to concentrate on their core functions: preventing and resolving issues within the monitored environment.

System automation and console operations cover the operating system and its related products. Message suppression and automated replies, pseudo commands (shortened versions of long or complex commands for a desired outcome), system shutdown and restart, tape operations, and application failure recovery are the main focus in this area. A console operator should never have to perform business-as-usual activities on a mainframe, midrange, or server computer system. Any interaction should be as a result of an alert that needs to be investigated. Everything else should be performed by automation or should be eliminated. Things such as status messages from an overnight batch process, which display informational messages to the console, can be eliminated or sent only to the output log and removed from the console. Messages from a batch process that say to enter "Yes" if a required file has been received can also be eliminated. Today most batch scheduling applications can easily perform that task. System automation can fill in for the few instances where the function cannot be done with a scheduling application.

Automated console operations provide the greatest benefits to the operational staff within the command center. That type of automation includes but is not limited to the following:

Message suppression and automated replies

Messages going to the operator and system consoles have multiple adverse effects. For one, they utilize system processing power that could be better served for customer transactions. Second, they tend to flood the monitoring screens, creating an opportunity for critical messages to be missed. The preferred method is to eliminate unneeded messages at the source, thereby reclaiming computer processing and storage used to create, display, and store them. If that is not possible, then automated message suppression can be used to prevent the messages from being displayed so that staff can better monitor the meaningful messages created during problems.

There may be certain system and application messages that cannot be eliminated. Some of those require a response, such as when a tape drive gets a read error or when certain conditions are met. Messages that require an operator response have the potential for causing extended delays if they are not seen and responded to within a short time period. Allowing those types of messages to exist is inviting trouble, and most can be eliminated through the use of proper scheduling, application changes, or as a last resort, through system automation.

That type of cleanup and automation:

1. Reduces the number of messages sent to the operator console. By reducing message traffic to the consoles, critical messages become more likely to be seen instead of hidden among hundreds of messages.

2. Responds automatically to messages, reducing the number of replies an operator issues. By trapping messages with standard replies, automation issues the reply immediately, creating faster throughput and increasing accuracy.

Pseudo commands, system shutdown and restart

Pseudo commands are created to allow complex procedures to be executed with a single command. For example, without automation it may take more than 50 commands to shut down all of the active tasks and applications on a mainframe system. Using pseudo commands, an operator would enter one shutdown command, triggering automation to perform each of the steps the operator previously performed manually in a fraction of the time. The same applies for system startup, especially after a system crash. An operator can initiate startup with a single command, or startup could be fully automated in case of a system failure, considerably reducing the length of an outage.

Many operator procedural errors occur when attempting to restart a failed mainframe computer system. That happens in a manually started environment, when an operator issues the start of day startup command for a critical online application, rather than the recovery mode called for after a failure. Automation can detect a system failure and issue the proper startup command, completely eliminating that common procedural error, which in most cases is visible to your customers.

Tape operations

Data centers that utilize manual or automated tape drives occasionally encounter read or write errors. When that happens, the batch process running at the time either fails or prompts the operator to select another drive to swap to. Automation can respond to those swap requests by determining whether any compatible drives are available, and if so, responding with the drive. Once the swap is completed, automation would then take the drive with the errors offline for diagnostics and create a trouble ticket.

Many delays in overnight batch processing are caused by swap requests, generated from a read or write error, that are not seen or responded to in a timely manner. Don't forget, batch processing for that application comes to a grinding halt until the swap request is satisfied. Automating the function reduces recovery time and further delays by taking the failing drive offline before another batch process grabs it, which usually happens when the task is performed manually. Automatically creating a trouble ticket allows for accurate tracking of failing drives through daily, weekly, and monthly metrics.

Application failure recovery

Every so often, for any number of reasons, an application crashes, similar to what happens on a PC. When that happens, your customers can no longer perform what they need from that application. You begin losing money, your customers become unhappy, and your help-desks get flooded with phone calls. In those situations, automation can be pre-programmed to perform recovery actions to get the application running again and your customers back doing what they need. The recovery process can be programmed to included diagnostic and restore steps and a specific number of retries. For instance, if automation attempts a restart and the application crashes again, automation can be programmed to stop or to try restarting the application a second time using different startup options.

Automated recovery usually gets the application back up and working again while most customers are just trying to get back into the system or even before they are affected.

Automated batch job scheduling and failure recovery

The purpose of automating scheduling changes and failure recovery is to aid development teams by reducing turnaround time and allowing for last-minute changes even for applications containing hundreds of modules, while reducing errors.

- Automated job scheduling from developer-provided documentation submitted through the change process eliminates keying errors and greatly reduces the number of resources required to implement scheduling changes. In fact, the vast majority of scheduling changes can be implemented automatically, without anyone having to intervene.

Automating the scheduling function reduces the number of change-related or keying errors during overnight batch processing. The improved speed and facility also allow rapid implementation of late-arriving application handovers that are critical to the business or to meet regulatory requirements.

- Automated batch failure restart and recovery can be used on many batch processes for failures that do not require complicated recovery actions, such as space or read/write errors. That eliminates the potential for human errors and delays while technical support looks up and performs recovery actions in order to resume batch processing.

Automated trouble (incident) ticket and report generation

With all of the tools available, there is absolutely no justifiable reason for anyone in a command center to create a trouble ticket manually for any alert-generated notification. Plain and simple: If the system can generate an alert and send it to a command center monitoring screen, there is no reason that the system cannot also generate a trouble ticket for the event.

Automating the creation of trouble tickets also allows for standards to be implemented so that meaningful metrics and reports can be automatically generated, all of which contribute to the incident and problem management processes.

Having a trouble ticket ensures every alert is tracked as part of the incident and problem management process. Trending reports help identify recurring problem areas, providing the opportunity to prevent repeat occurrences. Other benefits from automating trouble ticket generation include:

> The opportunity to implement automated notification and escalation.

> Alerts can be automatically cleared from the monitoring screens once the trouble ticket is resolved.

> Reduction of the number of resources required to monitor and react to alerts.

A word of caution when implementing automated ticketing: Filters and logic need to be implemented in order to prevent generating an excessive number of tickets for duplicate alerts or system failures. Creating an excessive number of alerts makes the process meaningless; they distort metrics and trending reports, hide real problems, and eventually become ignored by the support teams, who feel they are chasing ghosts and do not have the resources to manage such a high number of tickets.

Automated help-desk: self-service

The purpose of providing clients a self-service tool is to get the command center out of the service desk business and back to incident prevention through proactive monitoring.

As a result of their function and the access they have, command center staff may tend to get help-desk type phone calls. Some of those calls have to go to the command center as part of the console operator function, such as restarting a printer. The requests may seem harmless, especially when they happen infrequently. The problem occurs when the command center takes on additional workload. Over time, the calls increase to the point where the command center staff may miss critical alerts because they are busy taking those calls.

Turning calls and e-mails into a self-service process reduces staffing requirements and is simple enough to do. Unless your company is drowning in cash, IT management is focused on building a massive empire, or help-desk type nuisances are so infrequent, there really is no reason to have command center staff dedicated for that purpose. Almost any user calls, e-mails, faxes, and requests going to the command centers, tech support, or scheduling for common repetitive tasks can be made into a self-service process.

Requests that can be turned into a self-service process include:

- Trigger a scheduled job on request

  Rather than call the command center to begin end of day processing, business divisions can initiate end of day themselves, eliminating the need for an e-mail or phone call and possible delays to batch processing.

- Query system or batch job status

  At one shop, command center and scheduling staff devoted several hours each morning fielding calls from users, developers, and others looking for the status of a particular batch job. Four hours per day were reclaimed by offloading the scheduling data onto a database where users could query batch information for themselves.

- Requests for access to production

  Many places perform these types of access requests manually for technical support teams and developers attempting to diagnose active incidents. When the function is automated, it is usually the front end, where the request is taken, which is then handed off to an employee for manual processing. Though streamlining the request entry process helps, it does not go far enough in terms of reducing turnaround time, errors, audit exceptions, or staffing requirements. To implement the feature properly, both front- and back-end processing should be automated, removing the human interaction altogether on the fulfillment side, and all associated requirements and problems.

Real-time validation for those requests can be performed and logged automatically by the application, validating both the request and the person making the request. Some of the criteria that can be validated include:

> An approved change record

> A valid trouble ticket that must meet specific validation criteria

> Restrictions to a specific system, such as development, and for specific devices

> Restrictions to user's own ID and development batch jobs

Other requests that may not occur as often but distract staff from their core function include:

> Update batch process with user input

> Report recreation

> Device resets (terminals, printers, etc.)

> Cancel a development batch job

> Cancel or reset user IDs

> Start or stop a development task

When implementing a self-service tool, make sure the back-end process is automated. There are some tools that will only automate the front end while the fulfillment aspect remains a manual effort. But doing so does not go far enough. Most of the errors, delays, and need for resources are on the back-end fulfillment process. In order to implement a proper self-service solution, both the front-end request and the back-end fulfillment process need to be automated.

Automated daily exception reporting

Exception reporting helps keep you on track by letting you know when something stops working, rather than finding out later from others, or worse yet, from your customers.

Things change over time, and what is working now may not be working six months or even days from when it was first implemented.

One location thought everything was running great until a server hosting a critical business application failed after running out of space on the primary hard drive. The monitoring application had been configured to send an alert to the command center when space went below three specific thresholds. A review of the log files showed that no alerts were sent to the monitoring screens. Testing the monitoring application showed that it was not generating alerts. Further investigation revealed the monitoring application had stopped working several months earlier after security policy changes were made on the server.

That incident prompted a full review of the monitored environment, which revealed that monitoring was not working on 25% of the environment. Naturally, monitoring was immediately fixed on each of those devices.

To prevent a recurrence, a daily exception report was created that sent a notification to the device owner, the application manager, and the event management team for any production device where alerts were not being sent to the command center monitoring screens. It detailed the specific reason for the issue and the possible courses of action to correct it. A weekly summary exception report was also created and sent to the appropriate managers within each team.

The daily exception reports are a good way of informing the responsible party of an issue. The weekly summary reports ensure that management is aware of the issue in order to address devices where monitoring has not been fixed.

As automation begins to be implemented, metrics and reports become easier to generate and modify as needed, allowing for accurate daily usage and exception reporting as well as summary trending reports.

There are many benefits from incorporating automation into your command center functions. The main ones include:

For the businesses supported:

> Reduce the number of business outages

> Reduce the duration of business outages

> Timely notification of critical issues

> Improve service-level delivery to the customer

For development and technical support teams:

> Reduce the number of callouts

> Improve request turnaround time and accuracy, especially when the command center is busy and unable to take user calls

> Reduce time required for development and testing

> Reduce printer and other device downtime

For the command center:

> Improve goal achievement

> Reduce or eliminate preventable outages due to improved proactive monitoring

> Reduce outage duration for unavoidable outages, such as hardware failure or communications disruptions

> Additional systems and workload can be brought in without the need for additional staff

> Alleviate constant workload

> Improve contact list management

> Improve alert documentation

> Reduce the number of non-actionable alerts

> Reduce calls into the command center, allowing proactive monitoring of the environment

> Reduce fax and e-mail requests to the command center

Chapter Seven

Process Improvement

(Also known as Process Reengineering or Optimization)

Process improvement, process reengineering, and optimization are terms that refer to the act of reducing the resources required to perform a function or task. It is the act of making things run better, faster, cheaper, and with fewer defects.

If you remove an irrelevant step from an order processing system that saves 30 minutes per order, you have just made a process improvement. On the other hand, if you eliminated the order process altogether by enhancing the request process to automatically generate the order, you just eliminated days or even weeks from the procurement process. You just optimized your entire procurement system.

Though small individual process improvements are good and should be encouraged wherever possible, overall optimization should be the ultimate goal. Take for example a human resources system that needs 8 hours to generate the payroll for all of the employees within company A. What if one of the system developers finds a process improvement that cuts the time down to 7 hours? Under normal circumstances, that 1-hour savings would be a major improvement, but what if that payroll system is capable of completing the task in 4 hours? A process optimization effort would look at the entire HR system and not just one step within the payroll process to find the most efficient way for the entire system to run. An improvement here and there is fine if you are OK with the system running for 7 hours and you're not worried about expenses.

Remember, by optimizing the process and reducing the time from 8 hours to 4 hours, you have also cut in half the resources used, allowing another process to use those resources and possibly run quicker as well.

Process improvements that look at an individual process to see how it can be improved are fine if you have deep pockets and are only slightly concerned about expenses or growth. That notion no longer fits in with the current corporate climate of growth while limiting or reducing expenses. Though small isolated improvements can help certain processes and can result in some expense reduction, they do not go as far as they can or should.

The most difficult and crucial part of an optimization effort is determining the scope of the process under review. Review a subset of the entire process, and you end up with some process improvements. Capture too much in your review, and you end up with steps that do not belong together and a failed effort. For example, to document the process flow for making an egg breakfast, where do you start? Do you start with breaking the egg? Where did the egg come from? Do you start by getting the egg from the fridge? How did it get into the fridge? Do you start at the store? How about leaving your house to go to the store? What is the best starting point for the process flow?

Obviously, it is not an easy question, and it's the reason there are many small individual process improvements but very few entire process or function optimizations. That is what differentiates the standout companies for a given industry whose profit margins are higher than their competitors'.

The goal should be end-to-end process optimization, which encompasses an entire workflow from start to end. In order to achieve the end-to-end process optimization, there may be many small process improvements or one major reengineering effort. Some systems will be designed optimally, and you may only find a few small process improvement opportunities. Other systems may require a complete reengineering that may never happen due to budgetary considerations.

The first step in the process is to develop a flow chart of the entire workflow. The most important part of this step is to exactly determine the first step. Leaving out some of the steps and choosing the wrong starting point will make this a simple improvement rather than an all-encompassing process optimization.

Next is determining the last step in the process. Chose the wrong step, and your process will not be as streamlined as you would like it to be. Take the example of the egg breakfast again. When is it done? When the plate is in front of you? What about the juice or the toast? How about the napkin, salt, knife, and fork? If you were the cook, what would be your last step: placing the egg on the plate, ringing for pickup, or when the plate is actually picked up?

This example highlights the importance of finding the proper starting point:

The event management team at one shop was receiving many complaints for slow turnaround in implementing new monitoring. Application development and technical support teams were frustrated at the inability to get monitoring installed on new servers and applications in a timely manner. In some instances production rollouts were stalled several weeks until monitoring was enabled. In others they were placed into production without monitoring and alert generation enabled, leaving the business vulnerable to outages that could otherwise have been prevented.

Event management staff members were frustrated as well due to the refusal of management to hire additional staff to better manage the workload. Before agreeing to hire more workers, management asked the team responsible for development work in the monitoring tool, the engineering team, to see whether any improvements could be made to reduce the time to implement new monitoring.

The engineering team carefully reviewed the process performed by the event management team for new monitoring requests and was able to streamline it, cutting the time to enable new monitoring from an hour to 15 minutes, if no mistakes were made. Quite often, usually because of outdated documentation, a server administrator would install the wrong version of the monitoring tool. When that happened, enabling monitoring for that particular server and application would take days.

Once the improvements to the new monitoring request process were implemented, the two-week backlog for new monitoring dropped to one week.

Two months later the workload increased as the result of a hardware refresh. Within a few weeks after the refresh started, the backlog for new monitoring was up to three weeks.

A month later, the businesses complained to IT senior management about poor performance from the command center after problem management noted that several outages impacting large numbers of customers could have prevented if monitoring was enabled.

A process improvement team was called in, which performed a full review of the event management team and the on-boarding process. The team identified the start of the process as the point when a new server begins to be configured with the required operating system and software, and the end when the server gets classified as production in the inventory classification system.

The solution that was developed and implemented completely automated the entire process. Best practice monitoring profiles were created. The monitoring tool was tied into the inventory system and included into the standard build for each particular type of server, which meant that it would get automatically installed immediately after the operating system was installed.

Overnight, the backlog disappeared. With 75% of the workload eliminated, the event management team was able to reduce headcount by 25%, and utilize another 25% for process improvement projects. Application and support team members had more time to focus on their core functions because they no longer had to put in requests for new monitoring, install monitoring software, or remove an incorrect version, and then spend untold hours following up.

As you can see, though a small improvement will produce some benefits, it may not go far enough to make a big difference.

You can read more details regarding the above issue and what else was done to address the business complaint in Case Study #1 within chapter 10.

The best way to begin is to find a common factor with all of the individual parts you are trying to optimize. For some, that may be the change process. For others, it may be the approval process, the inventory system, or purchasing. Each optimization endeavor needs to address that very carefully, because the common factor is where most of the improvements and changes will originate and be the most effective. The common factor will determine what modifications need to be made to the other (or child) points.

If there is no common factor, then you need to examine whether the different interactions are really interconnected within the process flow or whether there is a step that should not be part of the process. If at the end of the review it is determined that all of the interactions belong together, then you've come to the first decision point; should one of the interactions be altered to become the parent, or common factor, and all others become sub points, or does a parent need to be developed? If there are already multiple interactions, each representing a different tool, to the process flow and none of them is going away, the last thing you may want to do is introduce another tool that needs to be developed, supported, and maintained. If one or more tool can be eliminated, then the savings achieved by the optimization effort will more than justify the introduction of a new tool.

A very important factor to remember with any optimization project is the KISS approach. Keep It Simple, Stupid; do not make it much harder than it needs to be. Avoid forming committees or large groups as part of the planning and investigation phase. They create a bureaucratic effect that greatly impacts the success of the project. The project needs to be driven by one person or a very small group (three or fewer members) with the authority to determine which direction to follow. Of course, they will need input from a large number of people and assistance from the different functions that are being analyzed, but the project leader must have high-level management support to make decisions that may upset some individuals.

When drafting your proposal, be sure to include the benefits for each optimization recommendation that you are making. What good will all your hard work be if your recommendations don't get implemented? In order for your optimization recommendations to work, they need to be implemented. There are several characteristics that will increase your chances of success. If you do not have them, you should learn to develop them: being persuasive, not taking no for an answer, and knowing how to escalate.

Your proposal should answer these six questions:

1. Who is affected?
2. What is the change?
3. When should the change be made?
4. Where should the change be made?
5. Why should the change be made?
6. How should the change be made?

Along the way, the project team will run into individual process or tool owners who do not want to cede any power. They will fight any effort that would encroach on their domain. They are either people who need to be in control or army builders who will see this as a threat to their power. The number of excuses they will come up with to prevent any outside automation or influence over their domain will be endless. For example, they will say things such as:

1. You cannot guarantee the integrity of the data.
2. This does not meet our compliance standards.
3. It's an audit violation.
4. Our system will become susceptible to data loss or corruption.
5. Performance will become unbearable.
6. It has to be done manually, otherwise people will forget what to do if automation breaks.
7. My management will not let me do this.
8. We do not have the resources or time to work on this.

Here is where the godfather effect comes in. In order to be able to get those optimizations implemented, you will need senior-level support. That support must be senior enough to overrule the objections like the ones mentioned above.

You will also run into managers who will have legitimate reasons for being unable to help. The biggest and most legitimate complaint will be lack of resources. Here you have several options for approaching the problem:

1. Volunteer yourself and members of your team to complete the required work.

   Clearly document what changes need to be made in a step-by-step flow chart-type document. Where possible, assign tasks to members of your team or to an outside team that has been tasked with supporting your optimization project.

2. Volunteer yourself and members of your team to perform day-to-day activities.

   If the work required is too technical or specialized and must be done by a member of that manager's team, volunteer to take on generic-type activities. You may not be able to free the required resources 100%, but you may be able to swap several hours here and there of your time for their time by doing certain non-technical activities.

3. Offer to have temporary help brought in to either perform the required changes or to offload day-to-day work to free up resources.

   Because the optimization project will have many significant long-term savings, whether in cost savings, customer satisfaction, or error reduction, senior management in most cases will not object to hiring a temp or two for a limited amount of time. The money spent will be more than offset by the improvements that will be gained by the endeavor.

In some cases, the goodwill generated by making the above suggestions may be enough for that manager to reassign his staffs' workload and to get your changes made.

If none of the above has swayed that manager, it is now time to approach his management to see whether that team's workload priorities can be adjusted or changed. There will be situations where none of the above will apply due to the nature of the work involved or management that is unable to prioritize the workload; there is simply too much work and not enough staff or time. Those will be departments that are simply overworked. Their workload is consistently increasing, but their staffing has not changed.

Look at things in their simplest manner. Don't try to overcomplicate a process that should be simple. Don't take no for an answer. Remember the KISS approach. Sometimes, it is better to be ignorant of the technical aspect or limitations of what you are looking at. When you hear statements such as "that can't be done," ask why not. If that particular product is not capable, is there any reason the product cannot be changed? If there is, maybe an interface could be developed that would accomplish the same goal. If it is an outside vendor or an off-the-shelf product, contact the company that developed the product. Most companies may develop your enhancement requests for a set fee. If the request has the potential to benefit other customers, you should be able to bargain a good discount in exchange for letting the vendor incorporate the enhancements into the next public release of the product.

Improvement Recommendations

Mainframe Systems
Identify all manual tasks

Review system log for operator entries.

> Unless it is to invoke business recovery, no one should be entering commands on the system consoles. Any that are made will show up in the system log.

Track all incoming phone calls.

> The only phone calls coming into the command center should be to report a current or potential problem. No help-desk type phone calls, such as to reset a printer or a user's password, should be made to the command center.

Review scheduling and application audit log for all manual operations.

Asking staff members to document all manual activities will only provide partial results. Some might be too busy to document everything, and others will do things on autopilot, not giving them much thought and not thinking they are worth mentioning. There will also be others doing "favors"—things they should not be doing—that they will neglect to document.

Identify batch failures by type

Utilize auto restart for all read/write-type errors and system failures for all jobs that can be restarted from the beginning without any intervening action.

Some automated scheduling applications have the capability to automatically restart a failed batch process based on the type of failure. Automated restarts, with a corresponding trouble ticket, reduce processing delays and prevent the chances for a tech-support mistake.

Adopt and enforce JCL standards for space utilization and other best practices aimed at reducing processing times and failures.

Standards also help to reduce errors during change implementation and quality assurance times because tools can be utilized to perform automated checks.

Ensure all datasets are managed by a space management package, such as SMS.

Using global data classifications for each type of space allocation eliminates the need for specific space allocation. For example, using dataclasses (small, large, etc.) reduces the number of space-related failures

Install automated trouble ticket generation and recovery actions where possible.

Simple production batch and started task failures are ideal candidates for automated recovery because they usually only require a straight restart without any modifications. For started tasks, automation can be tailored to attempt a specific number of restarts or to use different parameters before sending an alert to the command center monitoring screens.

Batch failures due to hardware errors occur from time to time. Automation can remove a device from service if there are any errors or take preemptive steps to correct the issue even before any failures occur.

In addition to performing recovery actions, automation can fully document the error and subsequent actions taken in the trouble ticketing system.

Identify all stops in batch process.

Utilize automation and scheduling application to eliminate stops in batch processes that are dependent on an operator action, such as startup/shutdown of tasks or the opening/closing of files. Elimination of those stops reduces the time required to complete nightly processing and prevents the possibility of someone forgetting to perform a required action.

Implement self-service process to enable users to set triggers.

For items such as end of day processing or reconciling totals, allow users to automatically trigger the continuation of processing rather than calling or e-mailing the command center staff to perform the function.

For example, some departments may require a proofing department to validate totals generated by batch against expected totals from clients to ensure all requires files have been received and processed properly. When satisfied with the results, a call is usually placed into the command center so that batch processing can resume. Rather than that two-step process, provide the proofing department a method where the approval automatically resumes batch, eliminating the need for the phone call and the risk of delays.

Convert manual check-off lists to an auto-updated real-time monitoring screen.

Almost every step that a person performs on a computer system to validate something can be performed by automation. Many of the tools have the ability to turn a status bar green if all corresponding checks are working properly, turn the status bar red if an exception is encountered, create a trouble ticket if needed, and send an alert to the monitoring screens.

Implement a Web-based self-service portal.

If your command center has turned into a service desk, a Web self-service portal might help return it to a monitoring and incident prevention center. There are many tools that can automate most of those functions, or you can have a tool custom-built for your specific needs.

Some of the processes that are ideal candidates for self-service are calls, e-mails, faxes, and requests to the command center, tech support, and scheduling teams for common repetitive tasks.

Here's a sampling of those types of requests:

- Functional (emergency) ID validation and release
- Test and UAT System and application startup or shutdown
- Initiate scheduled job on request
- Query system status
- Query batch job status
- Update batch process with user input
- Batch report recreation
- Device resets (terminals, printers, etc.)

- Cancel a development batch job
- Cancel user IDs
- Start or stop a development task

High-level overview of the process to follow with improvement opportunities

- Identify problem areas
- Determine objective
- Prioritize
- Map existing processes
- Identify roadblocks, solutions, and key players
- Map new process
- Determine how to implement and measure new processes
- Implement improvements

It may be a good idea to engage outside help when first looking to implement automation and process improvements. There are many consultants and consulting firms, large and small, that can help get started and help develop a process to continue the initiative.

Chapter Eight

Metrics (Statistics) (KPI)

Measuring what you do is almost as important as actually doing it. Metrics, the collection of key statistics or Key Performance Indicators (KPI), is how your performance is judged. Much like an employee's performance is measured by how he meets his goals, a command center measures performance by specific metrics. The proper metrics allows you to determine how effective your command center is and to measure the performance of one command center against another in a meaningful manner.

Metrics are also required in order to measure the effectiveness of a command center's process improvements. The use of proper metrics is crucial for showing the value derived from an effectively managed command center. Let's look at a case study in the use of metrics.

A company looking to reduce expenses hired consultants to measure efficiency. The efficiency experts came in and began handing out log sheets to each worker so that they could write down everything they did on a daily basis. The workers with the most time on their hands completely filled out the sheets, making sure every minute of the day was accounted for. Departments that were shorthanded had very little time to properly fill out the sheet, and as a result had many gaps in the log sheets. At the end of the efficiency review, departments that were shorthanded were told they had too many workers and needed to make cuts. Departments that were overstaffed were told they were very efficient and needed to make no cuts.

Two command centers were reviewed as part of that exercise. The first managed six mainframes hosting a handful of applications that were only required during business hours. It employed 60 full-time workers. The efficiency review consultants determined it was properly staffed and needed to make no cuts.

The second command center managed 50 mainframes hosting hundreds of applications, with operations that were required almost 24/7. Most of the applications were only unavailable for 4 hours on Sunday mornings, when all required system changes were made, and several that required 24/7 availability had to be moved to backup systems in order to implement any required changes. This command center had 40 full-time workers. The efficiency review company determined it was overstaffed and needed to make a 30% cut.

This is where you learn the value of metrics and how they can be manipulated to suit a specific need. The first command center produced metrics showing how much work they did. The second command center produced metrics showing system productivity. The first performed a lot of busy work, so measuring productivity would not have been very beneficial to it. The second measured productivity to showcase all the process improvements it made and how efficient it was. To outsiders, including the efficiency experts, the first command center was more productive and deserving of high praise.

For departments with multiple sites, the best practice is to standardize metrics and reporting across the board to ensure you are comparing apples to apples and oranges to oranges. The team performing the function should not be the same one determining what to measure and which metrics to produce. A separate team should be tasked with that as well as distributing the data and ensuring that metrics are applied equally to every team within command centers that perform the same function.

Here is a sampling of what to measure and report for an infrastructure command center:

Number of customers served by managed systems

The total number of customers served by the systems under your management is a very good metric to capture. That number is also helpful for trending. Keep in mind the numbers by themselves do not paint a full picture. Eight million customers on one mainframe computer is a lot more impressive than 8,000. However, that would not be true if the 8 million were individual customers and the 8,000 were corporate customers, each managing thousands of clients on your system.

Transactions executed and types

This number goes hand in hand with the number of customers and reflects the amount of activity generated by those customers. This metric would most likely show many more transactions being executed on the mainframe with the corporate customers.

Notifications and escalations

These numbers are difficult to collect if notifications and escalations are being performed manually. If they are automated, notifications should closely match the number of alerts. A high number of escalations should be of concern to management: the number reflects notifications that went unanswered and had to be escalated to the next level, as well as the number of times that an escalation had to be made to management when a support team member exceeded the time allotted to resolve an incident.

Alerts

This number represents the total number of alerts that were displayed on the command center's monitoring screens. In a properly configured command center, each one of those alerts generates work for the monitoring staff as well as for the support teams. A high number is a good indication of problems with the monitoring application or elsewhere in the monitoring process. High numbers usually mean that many non-actionable or false alerts are being sent to the monitoring screens, causing many to be ignored. That can be validated simply by looking at the monitoring screens and seeing whether they are empty or filled with pages of alerts.

Systems managed and supported, including locations and types

Regardless of the number of customers served, each system managed represents work for the command center.

Incidents

Incident information is very important for everyone, especially IT and business management. Incident information should include the number of incidents for each severity level; whether they were change related, recurring or preventable; the business affected; and the department responsible for the cause.

Outages impacting customers

These totals are usually summarized in the high-severity incident metrics. The cause, fix, number of clients affected, financial loss, duration, and other relevant information for each outage should be detailed for this report.

Changes performed

This is the number of changes affecting systems and applications managed by the command center. Included in this number should be a count of changes where the command center was actively involved. The second number represents work for the command center staff. Extreme care needs to be taken when deciding which change metrics to produce. It is best to capture the number of changes as well as the functional purpose of the changes. For example, an application change to add new functionality followed by four changes to make corrections may be counted as five changes, when in reality it is only one change and four corrective actions.

Statistics for any automation in place

These statistics represent how effective the command center is at process improvements and is a good way to toot your own horn.

Call statistics

Command centers should not receive a high number of calls. They are not call centers and in most cases should have more calls going out than coming in. A high number of incoming calls is a sign that some people might be using it as a call center or information desk. That should be a cause for concern for management.

Trouble ticket statistics (total, by automation, manually created, open, resolved, etc.)

These numbers would be the tickets opened manually by the command center staff, on its behalf by automation, or assigned to it. They are good metrics for the shift managers to review on a daily basis.

Batch processing statistics

These statistics should include the total number of batch jobs executed, the number of failures, the number of repeat failures, the number that missed their target end time, and any other relevant information.

Service-level performance

This is where a properly managed command center will shine. The numbers represent how well you've met your goals.

To ensure accuracy, the metrics should be collected and the reports generated automatically. That applies to daily, weekly, and monthly metrics.

A good practice is to have an internal reporting team that has the proper training, experience, and authority to create and sustain an effective metrics program charged with data mining, analytics, and reporting. That team would be solely responsible for reporting the data, and not for what the data is showing. Responsibility for the data would still fall on the shoulders of the individual teams to which the data applies. Remember, killing or rewarding the messenger for the content of the data ensures only positive results would be presented, regardless of the actual conditions.

Distribution of data

All command center metrics information should be distributed to the clients supported and be made available for everyone. There should be no hiding of metrics that put the command center in a negative light. The goal of providing metrics is to show reality so that senior management knows exactly what is happening within the corporation, good or bad.

It is for that reason that command centers should not be seen as the cause of the problem or be blamed for the poor performance of a managed system or department, merely because it is reporting the bad news. The command center is the messenger, and to ensure the data is always accurate and concise, do not kill the messenger.

To help ensure unbiased reporting and behavior, a good practice is for command center management to report to a chain of command that is not directly responsible for any of the environment being monitored.

Words of caution

The command center should not be tasked with reducing the number of incidents, except for those that should have been prevented through proactive monitoring. In order to ensure that every incident and outage is reported accurately and timely, it is best to task the command center with resolving incidents and outages as they occur. The problem management teams and the individual divisions should be responsible for providing a permanent resolution to outages along with the task of reducing them.

If possible, the command center staff should make recommendations about reducing or preventing outages to the business owners, but they should never be held accountable for the number of incidents. When the command center is held accountable, the number of high-severity incidents reported begins to decrease, while the number of low-severity incidents goes up, or they both go down. Customer complaints, on the other hand, begin to go up. That is one of the reasons that the proper metrics are crucial and that there be no conflict of interest in reporting the data.

Naturally, the command center should be held accountable for outages that occur because an alert was ignored. But even in those instances, the command center should not be held accountable for the outages themselves, only for the deficiency in monitoring. For example, if a server fails because the primary hard drive ran out of space, the command center would be accountable if an alert was generated but ignored, but the server owner would be responsible for determining why the drive ran out of space and for taking actions to prevent a future recurrence.

The number of incidents and outages is not a good indicator of command center performance. For example, a command center with a high incident volume may be a reflection of outstanding performance as more users call for incident management services, and a center with low volume may reflect poor service as users struggle with a problem, give up, or look for resolution elsewhere.

A highly praised command center in the midst of a business with a large number of customer complaints or low satisfaction is a sure sign that the proper metrics are not being collected, the wrong teams are being praised or held accountable, or a conflict of interest exists in the command center chain of command.

Chapter Nine

Alert Management

Alert management is the process of converting events that may cause a problem into automated recovery actions or alerts that are sent to the proper teams. Critical alerts for a production application would go to a command center, and alerts for a test system would go directly to the support teams.

Command centers usually do not perform monitoring for non-production or non-backup systems and applications. Those types of systems require constant interaction, which would divert the command center's staff from production-related events.

Guidelines for the alert management teams

Send only actionable alerts to the command center monitors.

An actionable alert is one that requires immediate action to address an anomaly that may lead to a failure of a system, device, or application.

Business leaders for one organization asked us to review a command center after one too many preventable system failures occurred within a short period of time. The command center monitoring screen was found to have hundreds of alerts, with only 25 visible and the rest up to 30 or more pages deep.

No wonder the business leaders were furious. Buried within those 30 or so pages of informational, test system, QA environment, change related, decommissioned, and other types of non-actionable alerts was an occasional alert warning of a critical condition, followed a short while later by an alert stating that the system had failed. The command center would learn of those system failures after customers began complaining.

Identifying the problem was the easy part. Fixing it was another matter altogether, requiring weeks of analysis, process changes, and automation initiatives, followed by the implementation of new controls and standards to prevent the problem from recurring.

Informational alerts have the potential to flood the monitoring screen, thereby causing real production alerts to move unnoticed off the main screen. Informational, non-critical, and non-production alerts should be sent to the owning groups and support teams rather than to a production command center.

Automatically generate a trouble ticket for each alert sent to the command center monitors.

For multiple related events, or duplicate alerts, implement thresholds and intelligence to avoid trouble ticket duplication or flooding of the trouble ticketing system.

Create a monitoring screen in one central location for the command center to view all trouble tickets created as the result of an alert.

Monitoring staff sometimes gets alert status and resolution updates from the trouble ticket. Providing them a screen with the latest trouble tickets eliminates the need for performing a search each time they need a status update.

The monitoring screen should include the alert description, status, trouble ticket system and number, assigned group, date, and time. Alerts should automatically update to ensure that the most current status is readily available.

For example, when an issue is resolved, the alert should automatically be removed from the command center view and moved to a "resolved" bucket. When a trouble ticket is resolved or closed, the corresponding alert should be updated accordingly.

- That also applies to events that are self-resolving (process restart or server auto-reboot) and to events that are corrected with manual intervention. For example, if a process fails and is automatically restarted, the process would no longer be down and the alert should not stay on the monitor. A trouble ticket should still be generated and assigned to the owning group in order to identify and correct the cause of the failure and to properly track the event.

Those requirements make it easier for the monitoring staff to determine which alerts require further action or escalation. They also reduce the workload for support teams, as well as the command center.

Implement intelligent alerting so that monitors are not flooded due to a single event or multiple occurrences of the same event, and to detect potential large-scale problems.

- A server failure should only result in one or two critical alerts encompassing the initial failure and all affected components.

- Display one alert for duplicate alerts, with a dynamic counter (where possible) showing the number of occurrences for the failure.

- Develop business rules to analyze events for patterns that could indicate a bigger problem or issue is about to occur.

Certain types of failures, such as a system failure, may result in hundreds of alerts being generated. In those types of situations, only one or a few alerts require action. The rest can be closed to remove them from view because the event that triggered the alert will automatically be resolved once the system is returned to service. A flooded monitoring screen in that situation will mask other problems that may have occurred as a result of the system failure. Eliminating the residual non-actionable alerts from view removes the need for the command center monitoring staff to determine which alerts require action and which can be ignored.

Implement procedures or business rules to establish manageable thresholds to prevent false alerts.

- Means should be provided for the reporting and remediation of false alerts to prevent recurrence.

If something is too much trouble to correct, the chances are great that it will be ignored or put on the back burner. Make it easy for system and application teams to correct improper thresholds, and you'll have a much higher success rate eliminating those non-actionable alerts.

Suppress alerts from being generated as a result of an approved change or a weekly operational activity, which normally occur during an applications defined downtime (Greenzone).

- Approved normal and emergency change requests must be accounted for in order to prevent false alerting.

Some scheduled changes require a system to be brought down or taken offline while the change is being implemented. If alerts get generated while that is happening, they are generally ignored.

The alerting system should be tied to the change system to automatically detect change-related outages due to normal and emergency changes and to suppress all alerts caused by such outages.

Monitoring and alerting should still be performed during Greenzones where no changes are being implemented.

Some changes implemented for application A may inadvertently cause a failure in application B. Knowing about that when it happens provides the command center time to have it corrected before the Greenzone ends, when customers will try using the application.

Archival system for alerts that includes sequential timeline of events, the decisions that were made and by whom, and the results/impacts of the mitigation/resolution.

- Reduces the time to resolve any alert that may recur at any point in the future.

In addition to alerts from the monitoring screens, other methods by which incidents are brought to the attention of the command center include:

- Calls received:

  > Outside call center or help-desk (customer care centers)

> Other command centers

> Other regions

> Systems support

> Application development

> Technical support

- Command center staff when they are unable to perform a function

Alert-reduction strategies

What often happens with monitoring and event management is that over time things begin to deteriorate. Initially, large resources are devoted to implementing an event-monitoring strategy, getting it to the point where events are detected and corrected before an outage can occur. Afterward, everyone moves on to other things, and before long there are too many alerts and too many outages.

It is very important when implementing a monitoring strategy to implement and enforce strict standards and rules, without exceptions or deviations. When standard exceptions are made, they tend to become permanent and are then followed by more exception requests. Before long, there will be more alerting exceptions than those following standards, rendering event management and the monitoring teams ineffectual.

- Automatically eliminate or suppress alerts during weekly downtime (Greenzone) for operational activities, such as backups, and approved changes.

- Provide the ability for system administrators and support staff to define and modify permanent recurring Greenzones using a self-service portal.

- Provide a one-time self-service process to automatically suppress and re-enable alerts for last-minute approved emergency changes.

- Provide the ability to create a temporary Greenzone within a request for change ticket, which is then automatically fed into the alerting application.

   That enhancement eliminates the need for event management staff to search, validate, then approve or reject change records that require alerts to be suppressed outside of the standard Greenzone, and then to manually process the request.

   When performed manually, about 25% of event management resources are devoted to that function. When automated, all manual processing related to those types of changes goes away. Additionally, with one less team required to review and approve records, the approval time for changes may be reduced.

   Accountability and audit tracking that associates the change record to the message suppression function for audit purposes becomes possible.

- Create an alert staging environment

   For new systems and changes, alerts should be generated and displayed on a staging monitoring screen for review by support teams before moving to production. Testing and non-critical alerts should be eliminated from the production consoles.

Command center staff should never ignore an alert or accept a request to ignore an alert as a valid response from the support teams. Every alert should have a corresponding trouble ticket and follow-up action to identify and correct the initial cause of the event that triggered the alert. The intent is to permanently resolve the event so that it does not occur again at a later date.

Automated ticketing

The primary purpose of automated ticketing is to ensure thoroughness and accuracy, not to reduce resource requirements, although that is a side benefit. Automated ticketing ensures a trouble ticket is created for every alert, it is assigned to the proper team, and it is resolved in a timely manner. Documenting the resolution process allows the information to be added to the known error database, reducing the resolution time should the same event recur.

Several points to remember when implementing auto ticketing include:

- Automatically generate a trouble ticket for each alert.

    Automation cannot distinguish between a real alert and one that can be ignored, so it will create a ticket regardless of the condition. Command center staff tends to sympathize with some support teams and may not create a ticket for certain alerts they are told to ignore, reducing the chances for the alerts to be corrected.

- Ensure filters are in place to prevent an excessive number of tickets from being generated for duplicate alerts or a single occurrence.

  Nothing renders a ticketing system useless more than the generation of too many tickets. When support teams cannot keep up, they simply ignore all tickets, forcing the team managing the ticketing system to perform mass closures on a regular basis.

- Clear alerts automatically from monitoring console once the corresponding trouble ticket is resolved.

  Ordinarily, for each alert the monitoring staff makes the initial contact for support, and then makes several more attempts in order to get status updates. That option saves the command center monitoring staff time, eliminating the need to get a status update from a support member who forgot to call back after the problem was resolved.

Automated callout and escalation tool

Most delays during incident management usually occur when attempting to contact support. There is either a delay in making the initial call, the wrong individual is called, or too much time is given to the primary on-call support person before moving to the next on-call person. Automating the functions eliminates all of those conditions, reducing the problem-resolution time.

A VRU (Voice Response Unit) for callouts and escalations

1. Automatically contacts the on-call person via cell or home phone for a given alert.

2. Enables business groups and support teams to maintain and update their own contact and escalation information in one central location.

3. Automatically calls the next contact as needed.

4. Escalates to the manager of that group and finally to the command center if an alert is not acknowledged.

Self-service

Implementing a self-service option for event management reduces the workload for the event management team, reduces errors, and improves the chances for non-actionable alerts to be eliminated by setting the proper thresholds and outage schedule.

Here are some of the services that can be offloaded to the tool:

- Requests for common repetitive tasks.
  - > Adjust thresholds
  - > Create or modify alert on call list
  - > Create or modify alert escalation list
  - > Customize monitoring for a particular application or device
  - > Implement temporary Greenzone for emergency changes
  - > Query status of monitoring for a particular application or device
  - > View monitoring errors
  - > View historical data for alerts

> Request access to monitoring screens

> Request high-level monitoring dashboards

Benefits

A good event management strategy will deliver many direct and indirect benefits for just about every team in IT.

- Improve service-level delivery to the customer
- Improve the change management process
- Improve weekly change activities
- Improve recurring weekly activities
- Improve contact list management
- Improve alert documentation
- Reduce the duration of business outages
- Reduce the number of business outages
- Reduce the number of non-actionable alerts
- Reduce the number of callouts
- Reduce calls to the event management team
- Reduce the time required for development and testing

Chapter Ten

Case Studies

The six case studies that follow describe actual problems in various command centers across the globe. In most cases, the solutions identified and implemented were based on key concepts from the preceding chapters.

Case Study #1

Poorly performing infrastructure command center

Management responsible for the data centers and corresponding command centers across three continents servicing areas that included Europe, the Middle East, and Africa requested help after the business division heads complained of poor service and unhappy customers. The command center was producing metrics that showed they were meeting their obligation of creating a trouble ticket and notifying support within 15 minutes for each alert, but service disruptions were occurring more frequently. Senior management within the business divisions was receiving an increasing number of complaints from customers who either could not access the firm's applications or were able to sign onto the application but its response time was so slow that they quickly gave up. The senior business heads were not happy with IT for several reasons:

1. They were hearing of the problems directly from the customers rather than from Operations.

2. Servers would fail, making the applications running on them unavailable. Management was even more upset after learning

that warning alerts were generated and sent to the command center but no notifications or actions were taken to correct the cause of the alert, leading to a system failure.

3. Application-generated critical alerts had been sent to the command center indicating something wasn't working properly, but developers wouldn't hear about those issues until much later, after customers began complaining.

A service agreement had been implemented as a quick fix after a prior compliant by the business divisions of poor service. At that time, it was found that notifications were not being made for a large number of alerts. Rather than performing a detailed examination of the issues, an agreement was reached between the two sides that a trouble ticket would be created and a notification would be made within 15 minutes following contact instructions provided by the support teams.

Initially, there was a noticeable improvement in service, but over time the number of alerts increased. The increase gave the command center staff no time to verify that notifications were being responded to or that alerts were being addressed.

Senior IT management wanted to know why there were disconnects between the command center staff, which showed they were meeting their service-level agreements, and the businesses, which were taking a hit on revenue as a result of the high number of outages and poor customer service.

With threats of outsourcing the data centers and command center operations from the business divisions, data center management needed a detailed analysis of the problem and a permanent solution in place as soon as possible.

Analysis

Because the command center claimed to meet its goal, the first step was to look at the goal itself to see whether it was aligned with the businesses objectives.

The command center's goal was to ensure a trouble ticket was created and notification was sent to support for every alert received within 15 minutes.

The first problem was the goal:

1. It was not a valid goal, but rather a service-level agreement. The command center had no stated goals and only one implied goal: to ensure the service-level agreement regarding trouble tickets and notifications was met.

2. The agreement was not aligned with the businesses objectives. In fact, the command center had no goals that involved satisfying the clients it served.

3. The command center's only obligation was to create the trouble ticket and make the notification, period. If the notification was never received, was ignored, or went to the wrong person, e-mail, or phone number, made no difference to the command center; it was irrelevant. Resolution of the alert was irrelevant as well. The only obligation was to create a trouble ticket and make the notification within 15 minutes of the alert appearing on the monitoring screens, regardless of whether anyone actually received the notification within that timeframe.

The next part of the analysis was to talk to all of the parties involved to hear what they perceived as the most pressing issues: alert (event) management, incident management, support teams, and the command center monitoring staff.

Alert (event) management staff concerns:

- Excessive workload—The alert management team was being flooded with requests for new monitoring, threshold modifications, monitoring removal, and a host of other alert-related requests from the support teams and the command center staff.

- Insufficient staffing—Staffing had not kept pace with increases in the monitored environment.

- Outdated tools—Staff processed work requests using Excel spreadsheets and a very cumbersome request process that most other teams had moved away from in favor of an automated self-service process.

In addition to monitoring configuration changes, several team members were devoted to reviewing and approving or rejecting change control records for applications that required monitoring changes. The workload increased substantially as the number of monitored systems increased, requiring staff additions each year just to keep the backlog down to a two-week level.

Incident management staff concerns:

Once notified of an outage, the incident management team did what was needed to restore service. The complaints here were:

- Most calls came directly from the help-desks after customers began complaining, instead of beforehand from the command center.

- Delays in reaching the correct support personnel due to missing or incorrect contact information often added hours to the incident resolution process.

- There was slow response from the command center when seeking operational support.

Support staff concerns:

The application and system support teams both had the same complaints:

- The support teams were being flooded with alert-related e-mails and trouble tickets from the command center. Initially the support staff investigated each of those alerts, but over time they were staying up all night investigating alerts that belonged to someone else, were for development servers and applications, or could be ignored because of improper settings. With no way to distinguish which alerts were valid, and to get some sleep, the support teams began ignoring all alert-related trouble tickets and e-mail notifications, responding only when called directly.

- Requests to the alert management team for alert modifications took weeks to complete or were never made.

- To enable or remove monitoring was a long, arduous process. For existing systems it was easier to leave monitoring as is and to instruct the monitoring staff to ignore alerts.

- Change requests were often delayed due to outstanding approvals from the alert management team. Numerous calls, e-mails, and escalations by the change creators were often required to get a change record approved before the cutoff window.

  > Change control procedures required the alert management team to review and approve every change request where a system or application was being

modified so that appropriate alerting modifications could be made.

Monitoring teams concerns:

- Excessive number of alerts. Almost seven alerts for every monitored system, for a total of 55,000 alerts per month, were going to the command center monitoring screens. At any point in time there were at least 15 pages of alerts on the monitoring screens, making it impossible for the command center staff to do anything more than open a trouble ticket and make the initial notification.

- Missing or incorrect contact information made it difficult to meet the 15-minute requirement.

- Constant alerts meant the monitoring staff was busy from the moment their shift began until it ended. The environment had become like a factory assembly line, with staff constantly repeating the same steps over and over.

- About 90% of the trouble tickets were closed by support staff with instructions for the monitoring staff to ignore the alert.

- Hundreds of alerts would flood the consoles from scheduled changes, making it easy to miss any valid alerts that appeared during that timeframe.

Problems identified

The main problem identified was the number of alerts (more than 55,000 per month) going to the command center monitoring screens. With 15 pages of alerts on the monitoring screens, it was impossible to determine which alerts were nuisance alerts and which required follow-up actions to prevent an outage or to restore service. Anything that goes beyond the first page becomes hidden, and in all likelihood will lead to an extended outage. Monitoring screens should be empty or close to it at all times. The more than 55,000 alerts signified serious problems with alerting and monitoring.

1. A look at alerts and event management revealed the following:

    *   An excessive number of non-actionable (false) alerts due to
        o   Improper thresholds
        o   Scheduled changes
        o   Decommissioned servers
        o   Test and development systems
        o   Pre-production testing

        >   Alerts during development testing were being flagged as production and showing up on the command center screens.

        >   Monitoring and alert generation was not implemented for many new production systems due to the alert management backlog.

2. No automation. All requests to add, remove, or modify monitoring and alert settings were manually performed and took over two weeks to complete. Simple threshold adjustments were treated as least critical and took longer than two weeks to complete or were completely ignored.

3. No linkage between the change, asset, and alert management applications.

4. No monitoring and alerting standards or best practices.

5. Monitoring was broken on 25% of the servers. As a result, no alerts were generated when any adverse conditions occurred on those servers or any applications hosted on them.

Solution

The majority of the workload for the alert management team was divided between reviewing change management records and adding or removing monitoring due to server changes.

Most of the alerts going to the monitoring screens were non-actionable alerts due to scheduled changes, improper asset management classification, or development system alerting.

Several courses of action were begun:

1. Create default best practice monitoring profiles for any new system. For existing systems with multiple profiles, a common default was created.

   a. With default profiles in place, monitoring could be automated for any new systems or servers added to current applications.

2. Create automation to integrate the asset management systems with the alert management system.

   a. Would automatically enable monitoring on new production systems.

   b. Would automatically enable or remove monitoring on servers added to or removed from existing applications.

c. Would prevent alerts for decommissioned and non-production systems from going to the command center production screens.

3. Create automation to integrate the change management system with the alert management system.

   a. Would prevent alerts caused by scheduled changes from appearing on the production monitoring screens during the change start and end times.

   b. Change records that required alerts to be suppressed no longer required approval or any action by the alert management team, eliminating a large chunk of its weekly workload.

4. Implement a new policy requiring a response from the appropriate support team for every production alert sent to the command center monitoring screens.

   a. The monitoring teams were no longer allowed to ignore alerts.

      i. Responses such as "Notify me when it reaches 90%" were no longer accepted. Action had to be taken to correct the condition causing the alert or the alert thresholds had to be modified to alert at the appropriate condition.

   b. Some of the alerts were caused by individuals implementing changes without an approved change record.

      i. This policy helped to tightened change management controls by highlighting unauthorized changes.

5. Automate trouble ticket creation.

   a. Trouble tickets would automatically be created for every production alert sent to the command center monitoring screens.

6. Automate alert notification and escalation to the proper support teams.

    a. Instant notification would be made by a Voice Response Unit to the on-call support member, with a call to the next person in line or to the team manager if there was no response. Final notification would go to the command center if no one from the support teams responded.

7. Integrate support contact and escalation information with the asset and HR management systems to ensure data is always current and accurate.

8. Create separate rules for production and non-production alerts.

    a. Production alerts would go directly to the command center monitoring screens with a corresponding trouble ticket and support notification requiring an immediate response from the support teams.

    b. Non-production alerts would go directly to the support teams. Alert processing rules would be configurable by the support teams to utilize the preferred notification methods and timeframes for each individual.

9. Create QA screens to prevent pre-production alerts from flooding production screens and to provide the opportunity to eliminate ambiguous and incoherent alerts.

    a. This would be where monitoring and alerts get tested, tweaked, and adjusted before a system or application is moved into production.

10. Implement command center shift turnover meetings that include managers from the outgoing and incoming shifts as well as the senior command center manager to highlight current ongoing issues that may not seem significant at the time but may turn into major problems if not addressed in a timely manner.

Follow-up

As the above improvements were being implemented:

- The number and duration of business outages began going down dramatically.

- Avoidable business outages were virtually eliminated, and the duration for all other outages was cut dramatically.

- Almost overnight, requests for new monitoring decreased from several hundred per week with a two-week backlog to a dozen or so. Alerting and monitoring became an automatic process once a system was classified as production in the asset management system.

- New monitoring requests had previously required the requestor to submit a form using a complicated Excel spreadsheet. Those forms were extremely confusing and required the requestor to guess the appropriate threshold settings. The formation of best practice standard profiles allowed automation to be implemented, which alleviated the workload for the support teams as well as the alert management team.

- By the end of the first year, the number of non-actionable alerts virtually disappeared from the command center monitoring screens.

- Over a three-year period the number of monitored systems increased by 600%, and the size of the alert management and monitoring teams decreased by 25%.

- The alert management team had enough resources to create detailed training courses for the support teams and to expand their offering for business and database monitoring, helping to further reduce other problems that may affect customers.

Case Study #2

Merging command centers under time, resource, and compatibility constraints

An acquisition brought onboard an outsourced small computer room composed of UNIX servers and a corresponding operations center. Shortly after the acquisition, it became apparent that the newly acquired company had serious service problems, mostly due to IT-related issues.

Analysis

Initial reviews of the site highlighted serious procedural issues, such as the lack of change, security, and operational controls.

The operations and development teams had full unrestricted and unmonitored access to the production systems and were implementing large-scale changes during business hours.

No hardware, software, or system monitoring was installed on any of the systems. Equipment failures in the computer room went undetected, until customers called to complain.

Rather than try to piecemeal fixes, the decision was made not to renew the outsourcing contract and to move everything in-house, where existing standards, procedures, and controls could be utilized. Unfortunately, by the time that decision was made, the outsourcing contract was about to expire, leaving only three months to complete the move.

Problems identified

1. The move had to be completed within three months.

2. Change and security controls needed to be implemented as soon as possible.

3. None of the staff from the outsourcing company were willing to join the new company, which meant that new staff had to be hired and trained within that three-month timeframe.

4. No automation, not even a scheduling application, was installed on the systems in the data center. Computer operators did everything manually using written procedures, tracking sheets, and e-mails to perform day-to-day activities.

5. The systems in the acquired data center were non-standard, which meant that any automation in use by the existing command center was not compatible and could not be leveraged.

Solution

A senior command center manager was sent to the newly acquired operations center to train and take over day-to-day management of the site. That manager would begin the process of verifying operational procedures and updating or creating those that were outdated or missing.

- Duplicates of all procedural and reference documents were made during the verification process and sent to the target command center.

The hiring process was fast-tracked to expedite the interview and addition of 10 senior system administrators with programming experience to replace the outgoing outsourced computer operators.

Learning the manual processes on the systems and performing them on a daily basis would give the new staff a head start toward developing the required improvements and automation.

- Temporary operations staff members were brought in on a month-to-month basis to aid with operational activities, allowing the senior administrators to focus on service improvements and automation.

Security access to production was revoked from operations and development staff. Technical support staff members were provided with access on an emergency basis, to be utilized only during the course of restoring service to customers.

Existing command center space, reserved for future growth, was utilized to house the new staff members.

Although no change management tools existed with the new acquisition, training was provided by the change management staff to the acquisitions development teams for short-term enactment of a manual change management process so that existing rules and controls could be implemented.

- Long term, those systems would be incorporated into the standard change management tools in order to reduce resource requirements and to provide automated reporting and auditing.

During the first two months, select staff members from the source operations center were flown to the target command center to train the new hires. On alternate weeks, select staff members from the target command center were flown to the source operations center for hands-on training.

During the second month, staff at the target command center began performing day-to-day functions, with operators from the source center on standby. The senior manager on hand documented any occurrence where someone went off standby at the source site to ensure it only happened once. By the start of the third month, there were no occurrences of anyone going off standby.

By the middle of the third month, complete operational control was provided by the target command center.

- Documentation and contact information had been updated to direct everyone to the target command center.

At the end of the third month, the outsourcing contract expired.

- All network connections were disconnected.

- Security access for the outsourcing staff was revoked.

Follow-up

Within a year, the systems were fully automated, allowing operators from the existing command center to take over day-to-day operational functions while the newly hired systems administrators were moved into advanced systems positions.

Case Study #3

Merging two command centers under a resource constraint

Due to budget cutbacks, a decision was made to consolidate two command centers that were located 600 miles apart and that were serving different types of customers and computer systems. The first command center, where all of the work was being relocated to, had 32 staff members who managed over 30 large IBM mainframe systems and about a thousand servers, all of which were completely automated. The second command center, the one being closed, managed eight large IBM mainframe systems, 500 servers, and 100 older midrange mainframes, with just over 60 staff members. Anyone willing to relocate from the second command center would be given a job in the first one.

When moving a command center—or for that matter, any site—over large distances, there will be many staff members who will choose not to move. When the decision to consolidate was made, the economy was still experiencing tremendous growth and well-paying jobs were not very difficult to find for experienced workers. As a result, of the 60 or so command center employees, only four agreed to move.

Analysis

Staff within the first command center relied on automation and monitoring applications to perform routine day-to-day activities. Rather than rely on notes, memory, and tracking sheets, they relied on exception alerts from automation and the monitoring applications.

Staff within the second command center utilized notes, memory, tracking sheets, and detailed written procedures to perform day-to-day activities for the IBM mainframes, servers, and older midrange computer systems. The mainframes and servers utilized the same system software as those managed by the first command center. That meant the automation and monitoring applications used by the first command center were compatible with systems manually managed by the second. That provided the opportunity to get the automation and monitoring applications and rules installed and utilized, allowing staff at the first command center to manage the systems with minimal amounts of training and staff.

The problem was going to be the midrange systems. Staff at the first command center had no experience with those types of systems.

Problems identified

1. Only four staff members were willing to relocate from the second command center.

2. There was a lack of midrange experience in the first command center.

3. There was no automation or monitoring on any of the computer systems managed by the second command center staff.

Solution

The move was broken down into two phases, one for the midrange operators and the other for the mainframe and server operators.

Midrange

A third command center, located between the other two, was added into the mix. It had 15 staff members and managed several midrange systems. The eight staff members who managed the midrange systems agreed to make the move to the third command center.

1. Workstations with the required applications for staff to manage the midrange systems were configured and installed.

2. Connectivity to the midrange systems was established and tested.

All staff members were brought in on an off day to the third command center to ensure they were able to perform day-to-day functions without any problems. Once all eight validated that everything was functional, a date was established to perform phone transfers.

When the date arrived, the midrange operators from the second command center reported for work at the third command center. All midrange phone calls were automatically forwarded to the third command center.

Mainframe and server

Automation applications for message handling, suppression, and workflow automation were installed on the mainframes and servers being managed by the closing command center.

The monitoring applications and associated rules were installed on the servers and mainframes. Alerts generated were then incorporated into the monitoring screens utilized by the first command center.

Once the standard tools utilized by the first command center were fully functional on the systems managed by the second command center, a target date that allowed four months to complete the move of all functions was set.

- That timeframe allowed enough time for training, identifying and documenting any gaps in processes, and the HR termination process.

The contact information from the closing command center was merged into the applications being used by the first command center.

Standard security controls in place at the first command center were implemented on the systems managed by the closing command center. Security access was granted to the first command center staff on the mainframes and servers.

- An analysis was performed to determine any gaps in access required to perform day-to-day and emergency functions.

- A second analysis was performed to ensure all granted access met current security standards and controls.

Two staff members per shift from the closing command center were sent to the other site to train staff members on the corresponding shift.

- With standard tools, processes, monitoring, and online documentation in place, staff members at the first command center were able to manage the systems almost immediately.

The four staff members from the second command center who agreed to move were transferred to different shifts within the target command center, ensuring all four shifts had someone from the second command center.

For a two-week period, all mainframe and server operational functions were performed by staff within the first command center with staff at the second command center on standby.

Because no problems were encountered during the pilot test, the move was performed as scheduled.

- All phone calls to the mainframe and server operators were automatically transferred to the first command center.
- All functions became the responsibility of the first command center.
- Daily, weekly, and monthly metrics reports were expanded to include data from the newly managed systems, provided by the monitoring and automation applications.
- Security access was revoked for the remaining staff at the second command center.

Follow-up

Over the next few months, the number of incidents that affected customers began to decline on the systems moved to the first command center. With metrics reporting in place, staff members were able to begin process improvement projects on those systems, helping to reduce delays that had often occurred during overnight batch processing.

Case Study #4

Merge four large command centers into two sites

As a result of growing demand for data center space and to meet new government regulations regarding the location of primary and backup sites, a decision was made to consolidate four command centers. Those four command centers were the result of several mergers that were finalized at the business level but not yet integrated at the technology level. Each command center performed the operational functions for different data centers. Two also performed disaster recovery functions for each other but were only 10 miles apart and did not meet federal guidelines regarding the proximity of a backup site. Those command centers consisted of:

1. Command center 1 had 40 staff members who managed 38 large IBM mainframes and 2,000 servers across four data centers spread throughout the U.S.

2. Command center 2 had 64 staff members who managed 20 large IBM mainframes across two data centers. It was located in a data center and needed to move so that the space could be utilized for computer equipment.

3. Command center 3 had 36 staff members who managed 8,000 servers across two data centers. It was located in a data center and needed to move so that the space could be utilized for computer equipment.

4. Command center 4 had 72 staff members who managed 16 large IBM mainframes and approximately 1,000 servers across two data centers.

The command centers had to be merged without any disruptions in service, while maintaining backup capability and meeting federal regulations regarding distance between sites.

Analysis

Command centers 1, 2, and 3 were located within a 10-mile radius. Two were across state lines, but there was access to public transportation and available parking.

Command centers 2 and 3, which backed up each other, were using badly needed data center space and had to be moved as soon as possible. Data center space is extremely expensive and is not very easy to find, unlike command centers, which can utilize just about any type of securable space. Advances in mainframe technology eliminated the requirement to house operational centers nearby. The best strategy was to duplicate the site requirements at the other locations, then move all staff members. Any improvements, automation, or cross-training would be performed after the move.

The two sites also had specialized computer equipment with custom applications. Most of the equipment and applications could be duplicated, except for two pieces of hardware, a primary and a backup, which would incur a huge expense to duplicate. It was decided to move those rather than incur the expense of duplicating them.

Problems identified

1. Site 1 did not have enough space to accommodate the incoming staff and workload.

2. Site 4 did not have enough video wall space to accommodate the additional monitoring screens required.

3. Due to timing requirements and political in-fighting, no system or staffing changes were to be made during the mergers.

Solution

The strategy was to move all staff and primary functions from sites 2 and 3 to site 1 and their backup functions to site 4, which was halfway across the country.

An architectural firm with command center experience and a command center integration firm were hired to help with the expansion of sites 1 and 4.

Command center 1 was expanded by approximately 150%. Adjacent space that was being used to store backup tapes (which were shipped to another facility) provided enough room to add two additional video walls and corresponding operator stations. The site was laid out in an oval format, with operator stations and video walls on the two long and the far sides, manager offices capable of seeing all three in the middle, and the secured single entry portal at the fourth side.

Command center 4 had enough operator stations but not enough video wall space. With the help of an integration firm, the existing video wall, which used outdated overhead projectors, was dismantled and replaced with state-of-the-art video cubes. The new video wall was four times larger, providing enough space for the merger and future needs. The wall was upgraded in stages so that monitoring screens were always displayed.

When construction was completed, the required computer equipment was built and installed using specifications from command centers 2 and 3, with added redundancy for network, power, and computer failures at each station.

Sites 2 and 3 used VoIP phone systems, so duplicating those systems was fairly simple and straightforward. When the phone systems were in place, any incoming calls to those centers would also appear at site 1.

The backup from the custom-built system that couldn't be duplicated was moved to site 1. The company that built the system was then brought in to configure it for the new location.

When all of the equipment was fully configured, staff members from each site were brought over in stages for pilot testing. Every staff member was required to visit site 1 to test access into the building and the command center, and access into the computer systems and every application required. Due to the large number of staff members and several problems that were identified and corrected, the pilot stage took about one month to complete, which was within the project timeline.

Several staff member from sites 2 and 3 who volunteered to relocate was flown to site 4 to complete pilot testing.

When the equipment was fully tested and all of the problems were corrected, operators from site 2 began reporting for work at site 1. The transfers were performed over a two-week time period so that someone was always available at site 2 in case there were problems that required a fallback. No problems were encountered, and the move was completed without any user ever realizing that the entire command center had been relocated.

Next, the backup from the custom system was made into the primary and managed by staff from site 2 at the new location. The old primary was then shipped to site 4 and configured by the vendor to be the new backup.

Staff members who agreed to relocate were then transferred to site 4. Once they were in place, the workload was moved from site 3 to site 4. After a two-week period, with all work being performed by staff at sites 1 and 4, all remaining staff at site 3 was moved to site 1.

Sites 2 and 3 were left as is for a two-week period after all staff members and functions were moved, in case of serious problems.

After that period, sites 2 and 3 were dismantled and the space was reclaimed for data center use.

Follow-up

Disaster recovery testing was performed to ensure that each site was fully capable of supporting and performing the entire workload.

After the moves were finalized, a complete reorganization was performed that put all command center functions under a single senior manager, clearing the way for process improvements from each section to be leveraged into creating best practice tools and standards that would be implemented across the board.

Case Study #5

Business command center

The CEO for a very profitable business requested help due to an increasing number of complaints from important clients regarding poor service, delayed transactions, or systems that were unavailable. The CEO was frustrated at the lack of progress from the business command center in implementing monitoring that would detect and correct problems before customers were affected or that would prevent problems from occurring. The goal was to reduce the problems and to ensure senior management knew about any outstanding problems before the clients did.

Objective

1. Work with business command center management to improve proactive monitoring.

2. Reduce the number and duration of all customer-impacting problems.

3. Ensure senior management is aware of business impacts as they occur, before the customers realize there is a problem.

   a. Management wants to be able to call clients to say there's a problem being addressed, rather than have clients catch them by surprise regarding an ongoing issue.

Analysis

A review of critical business outages for a three-year period found the following:

1. The number and duration of the outages was growing by double-digit percentages each year.

2. Close to 50% of the outages were due to scheduled changes performed by the IT division, with a large percentage attributable to the developments teams.

3. Fifteen percent of the outages were recurring issues that weren't fixed until two or three occurrences.

   a. Many problems that affected customers were never documented, even though clients had complained and problem resolution (post mortem) notifications had been sent out.

4. A large number of outages caused by IT changes and upgrades or that were recurring issues were not properly classified. The cause was noted in the text fields of the corresponding trouble ticket, but the fields to flag the cause as change related or recurring were never checked.

   a. That meant metrics produced by the command center were inaccurate and unreliable.

A review of the business command center found the following:

1. There was no proactive monitoring.

   a. Command center management had stopped performing any proactive monitoring, focusing instead on reactive and support functions, and metrics.

2. There was selective tracking and reporting of business impacts.

a. A large number of problems were never tracked in the problem management system.

    i. Without problem management records, there was no way to determine whether the problems were fixed properly. Without a record of how a problem was fixed, each future occurrence required detailed analysis to resolve the issue, elongating the outage duration.

b. There was no automation: Everything in the command center, including metrics produced, was performed manually.

c. There was no problem management team.

    i. The reporting function of problem management was performed by the command center staff, but the analysis to determine the root cause and to implement corrective actions to prevent similar occurrences was not performed by anyone.

d. There were no standard, unbiased metrics.

    i. The metrics produced presented IT in a good light and failed to show any of the outstanding problems.

3. There was a lack of cooperation from the development and help-desk teams.

a. During conference calls everyone promised full cooperation but never followed through.

All of the issues were symptoms of an underlying problem. Unless it was resolved, addressing them individually would be like putting a Band-Aid on someone bleeding from broken bones.

The underlying problem was a conflict of interest between the command center and the teams it was supposed to watch over and report on. Though the stated goals of the command centers were aligned with the business goals, the actions of the staff were geared toward presenting IT, which included development and the help-desks, in a good light.

When the business command center was developed, it reported into the business division. Over time and several reorganizations, the command center was moved and began reporting into the development team. The unwritten goal had become to present the development teams in a good light. Proactive monitoring, which had previously been effective, was dropped in order to reduce the spotlight on the main cause of problems that affected customers: changes made by the development teams.

Recommendation

A command center should never be put into a position where a conflict of interest may exist. Senior management responsible for managing all business command center activities should report either into the business divisions they are responsible for monitoring or into an independent third party.

When the conflict of interest (and thereby all obstacles to full transparency) is removed, progress can be made with automating all manual functions, removing non-core development-related functions, implementing proactive monitoring, and building an independent problem management team.

- An independent problem management team would also serve to ensure full transparency and disclosure of events as they occur.

- Proactive monitoring, automation, and proper problem management would:
  - > Help to identify the root cause of the failures
  - > Reduce the outage durations
  - > Reduce the number of recurring issues
  - > Present senior management with a reliable view of problems and their true causes

Case Study #6

Late customer statements

Over time, as a result of growth and acquisitions, the number of customers increased. That's a problem most companies would love to have. As the number of accounts increased, the mainframe systems were upgraded to keep up with demand. Unfortunately, there is only so much computer hardware that can be added before it is no longer effective. At some point, especially with older programming code, increasing the processing speed, disk size, and memory size will no longer have any effect on how long an application takes to complete. In order to take advantage of new computer advances, such as multi-threading and other complex enhancements, many of the older programs need to be completely rewritten, usually at a massive cost and at the expense of development work for other critical enhancements that business divisions require in order to keep growing.

That point was reached for the applications that produce daily, weekly, and monthly customer account statements. Late weekly and monthly statements became the norm. Daily statements were completed on time about 75% of the time if no problems were encountered during batch processing. On nights were problems were encountered, the daily statement were late 100% of the time.

The application development teams were facing intense amounts of pressure from senior management to address the late statement delivery problem. After six months of tweaking existing code and making other performance enhancements, they were able to achieve only minimal improvements, reducing the delays slightly but still incurring delays nonetheless.

After the improvements, on occasions where all processing was perfect and without problems, weekly customer statements were shipped about a day late. On occasions where processing encountered problems, weekly statements were delayed two or three days and monthly statements were over a week behind schedule.

The development teams' senior management was frustrated and unable to dedicate staff to perform a full rewrite of the statement applications at any point in the near future, so they asked the command center process improvement team for help.

Objective

Deliver customer statements on time.

Analysis

The statement applications consisted of daily, weekly, and monthly streams, each of which was triggered when the prior stream was completed. A process similar to the theory of constraints was utilized to flowchart the entire statement process to determine bottlenecks.

One analysis found that when daily statements were on schedule, weekly statements executed during the weekend, when computer processing was at the lowest peak. If delays occurred, the weekly process would extend into weekdays, at a time when utilization was at the highest peak, causing the statement process and all other processing occurring during that timeframe to take much longer than usual to complete and leading to delays in other applications. The same occurred with the monthly processing, except that usually had a more adverse impact on other processing.

The flowcharts revealed that the majority of statement processing was single streamed, meaning that each process waited for the one before it to completely finish before it could start. There were very few statement applications that were able to execute concurrently. A review of durations found many variations in process durations.

Theoretically, statement processing should take the same amount of time for each run for a given number of accounts. Some variations were caused by processing bottlenecks, but the vast majority of the extended durations were found to be caused by limitations in the input/output subsystem. That was the part of the mainframe that read or wrote data. Statement applications process a tremendous amount of data, and any bottleneck in reading or writing that data will have an adverse effect on everything. In many instances, those bottlenecks would double or triple the duration, leading to the delays in delivering statements.

Two large files were identified as being used by the majority of the daily, weekly, and monthly statement processes. The name and address file was utilized the most, followed by the history file. Almost every statement batch process with extended durations, caused by the input/output bottleneck, utilized one or both of those files.

Another bottleneck was caused by the files themselves. Because those files were very large, they were stored on physical cartridge tapes, which meant they could be used by only one application at a time.

The third bottleneck was the main batch job (the collection of application programs that process data), which created the daily statements. The batch job duration fluctuated between 1 and 4 hours. In addition, everything in the statement processing workflow was on hold waiting for the batch job to complete. On closer observation, the batch job was found to be comprised of many steps, each creating statements for a specific business category.

The fourth bottleneck was tape read and write errors. Due to the size and heavy usage of the files, read or write errors would occur from time to time, stopping the entire statements process until a new set of files was recreated.

Solution

Mainframes have the capability to utilize virtual storage, similar to flash memory, for data that are heavily accessed. That type of storage is expensive and is usually reserved for smaller files. That solution was never previously considered for the files because it works only with files stored on disk; it doesn't work with files stored on tape or cartridge. With the price of storage much lower than it used to be, additional storage was acquired for those files.

The first change was to create the files on disk rather than on tape. That change was very simple and had an immediate effect on processing, providing a 15% improvement. Shortly afterward, the files were added to the virtual storage management application, which loads the most frequently accessed parts of the files into memory. That change is transparent to the statement applications; the files and processing work as before, but the effect of the change was the elimination of the input/output bottleneck. That provided an additional 10% improvement, but more importantly, process duration became more consistent.

With those changes in place, it was then possible to modify the flowchart of the statement processes. Batch processes, which previously had to run one at a time because the files they needed were on cartridge, could now be read concurrently. Five batch jobs, which collectively took 5 hours, were now completed in 45 minutes after the changes.

The next change was dividing the batch job that created the daily statements into separate smaller jobs. With the files stored in virtual storage, the smaller jobs were able to execute simultaneously, allowing all of the jobs to complete in 20 minutes. That allowed the next set of jobs in the workflow to begin executing immediately after the corresponding prerequisite job completed, rather than having to wait for all of the jobs to complete.

Delays due to read and write errors on the tape media were virtually eliminated. If there was an error when creating backups of the files to tape or cartridge, the backup process would be restarted without any impact to the rest of the statement batch that was processing.

After the changes were implemented, daily, weekly, and monthly statement processing began completing ahead of schedule.

Follow-up

Unintended consequences: As a result of the changes to the statements batch, other batch processes that often became delayed due to the heavy processing and input/output requirements of the statement jobs began completing earlier than usual.

Closing

There are two moments when a command center really shines: when it's first implemented and during a major crisis.

When a command center is first implemented with the proper functions, tools, standards, controls, and management structure, business heads will see the fruits of those changes in trending reports. They'll see reductions in customer complaints and expenses with a corresponding increase in revenue. Senior IT managers will see improved system availability, quality indicators, and a more productive workforce.

A command center really shines during a crisis because it becomes visible to senior leaders, unless that crisis was caused by command center staff. Watching an efficient and properly implemented command center perform crisis management is poetry in motion. Notifications and escalations occur like clockwork. Everything that happens is fully documented. No stone is left unturned until the crisis is resolved, and even then the focus shifts to prevention.

Unfortunately, those moments are few and far apart. Over time people tend to forget or move on, only to be replaced by new senior managers who are unfamiliar with command centers and their benefits or history.

Problems for command centers usually occur when new management, unfamiliar with automation and unaware of the former environment, comes along and begins making changes. Staff members who monitor screens are seen as sources of labor for other workloads. The ramifications of any changes do not become apparent immediately but slowly over time. More importantly, the first to take notice will be business leaders as customer complaints begin increasing.

Many times command centers become doomed by their own success. That happens mostly when management fails to promote the achievements made or outages prevented by the command center. What then happens is that other departments take credit for the results of improvements made by the command center, and it slowly changes from being proactive to being reactive.

Command centers also run into trouble when apples to oranges comparisons are made between a manual and an automated environment. The comparisons tend to be made on the amount of work being performed rather than how productive the work is or the size of the environment. At first glance, a command center with five staff members monitoring alert screens will appear less productive than a team of 10 staff members busily entering commands on keyboards and filling out forms. The fact that 30 mainframes are being monitored and operated by the command center with five staff members per shift versus four mainframes by the command center with 10 staff members becomes irrelevant.

Many of the issues can be mitigated with the proper metrics, which should include the number of outages and major events prevented from happening, and the promotion of process improvement achievements. Both of those need to be regarded as critical as every other function within the command center.

In addition to service improvements, a properly implemented command center can reduce the cost of IT, improve the success rates for data center relocations and consolidations, and reduce the time required to absorb new acquisitions. Consolidating command centers reduces risk and downtime by eliminating any confusion of whom to call for incident management and by allowing standards and best practices to be seamlessly transitioned to new incoming systems.

A little extra time spent in the planning stage can help ensure your command center will be a valuable resource to the company. A command center without the proper functions will never be as effective as a properly implemented one, regardless of how much monitoring is performed.

Showing how successful the command center is by creating and distributing the right metrics will get backing and support for it from senior business and IT leaders. Promoting the improvements driven and outages prevented by the command center will help ensure that as time goes by and new management comes along, it is able to remain a driving force for standards, best practices, automation, and more importantly, proactive monitoring.

Epilogue

Global Financial Holdings has been in the news headlines every day since Wednesday morning, with reporters and customers asking whether the global bank had become insolvent. Except for most of the people in Texas, almost everyone else in the country sees those headlines, including Secretary of the Treasury Ben Heyward.

Heyward didn't get that far in his career by waiting to see how things played out. When he first read the headlines regarding Global Financial's computer problems, he suspected things might be worse than they seemed. His fears are confirmed by Wednesday afternoon when the company's CEO, Victor G. Capistrano, a friend since college, calls to fill him in on the bank's problems and to ask for a favor.

Both men know that the regulators would be breathing down Capistrano's neck by the next morning if the systems are still unavailable. He asks Heyward to play interference, to buy Global a little time to get things working.

The minute they hang up the phone, Heyward dials Sharon Lazinby's number. As the chairwoman of the FDIC, it's her job to decide what will happen to Global should it come to that.

Heyward and Lazinby then hold a private conference call with their most trusted advisors to decide the course of action should Global fail to restore service. The decision is made to approach the head of TAG Bank Holdings, Steven Van Olsen, about taking over Global Financial. TAG, the largest financial holding company, is known for having the most efficient IT division in the industry.

The next morning Lazinby and Heyward meet privately with Olsen and Paul Hamilton, TAG's CIO, and explain Global Financial's data center problems. They want to give him several days to formulate a plan before he gives them an answer.

Olsen looks over to Hamilton, the architect behind TAG's technology strategy, who asks one question: What is the status of Global Financial's computer systems and backup tapes?

Heyward is unable to contact Capistrano, so he instructs FEMA to send staff to each data center to get a status report. Within two hours he learns that all of the equipment in each data center is operating normally using generator power, and all data backups have been completed and are ready to be shipped out for offsite storage.

When Olsen and Hamilton receive the information, they have a private meeting. Two hours later, Olsen provides his acceptance of the takeover: TAG will take control of Global Financial immediately once the go decision is made. Customers will have access to their accounts within three days of the takeover.

The hurricanes have disabled one of TAG's command centers and one of its data centers. Over the years, TAG has consolidated equipment into three large data centers spread out across the country and staff into three command centers strategically placed far from the data centers and close to large metropolitan areas.

Staff members at the two remaining command centers pick up the workload without any impact and immediately begin recovery procedures to restore applications affected by the crippled data center. Within two hours, all applications have been recovered and everything operating seamlessly using the two remaining data centers. Most customers are not aware that there's an outage. Staff members from the Dallas command center and the Houston data center are given the rest of the week off to focus on taking care of their families and to be available for volunteer efforts.

Seven days after Global Financial became unavailable, Mike Silverman, the company's temporary head of technology, calls Capistrano to inform him that the computer equipment moving company is having trouble mobilizing enough staff members to perform the move for Global. The move will require at least six members, and so far the moving company has managed to get two. The rest of the teams in Texas are busy working with FEMA and the utility companies to restore power and communications. But they do have two available members on the West Coast and three in Florida.

Capistrano authorizes the additional expense to the moving company and then hangs up the phone knowing he will soon be out of work. There is no more time. He had delayed calling Anderson and the Feds, hoping that things would look better over the weekend. But this latest news reinforces his feeling that it's all over for Global Financial. The calls need to be made now.

Capistrano places the first call to Heyward. His heart sinks when Heyward tells him they have a plan to restore customers' accounts by handing over his bank to TAG Bank Holdings and that Lazinby has a press release ready to go. The call ends quickly, and Capistrano is somewhat relieved. He can take that vacation his wife has been asking about for the last four years.

Within minutes the press release is made and the go decision is given to Olsen.

Working with FEMA, the Department of the Treasury, the governor's office, and local officials, armored trucks are sent to each data center to pick up and transport all backup tapes to the TAG data centers. Cars are sent to Global's technical staff for transport to TAG's command centers. The plan to move Global's equipment is canceled.

High-speed satellite dishes are installed on the roofs of each of Global's data centers and patched into its network. Any data that can't be restored using the backup tapes will be taken real-time using the satellite links.

Three days later, Global's main computer systems are restored using equipment in TAG's data centers. Testing confirms that ATMs are working and that customers can access their applications. Work will continue over the course of the next few days to fix problems as they occur, but for the most part Global Financial Holdings is back, rebranded as TAG Global Financial.

About the Author

Abdul Jaludi has 28 years' experience with command centers in the financial services industry. He has espoused and championed operational and monitoring efficiency as a crucial element in successfully and consistently meeting customers' needs and expectations. Facilitating 24/7 stability and availability within the unforgiving business environs of intense competitive pressure and strict regulatory requirements has been an ever-changing trial throughout his tenure. Nevertheless, it is within those challenging and high-stakes environs that Jaludi has become a successful leader.

His contributions include helping establish one of the most efficient mainframe banking environments in the world and leading many innovations that have become the global standard within his former organization. His accomplishments include department, function, process, and tool innovation and optimization. He transformed operations from a manual paper-based platform into a fully automated process long before automation tools were available or were thought practical or even possible. Jaludi has performed numerous command center audits to identify and correct reasons for customer dissatisfaction. His work included a full review of monitoring, overnight batch processing, incident alert notification, incident and problem management, and customer-service reports.

He has also completed many command center consolidations, usually a byproduct of mergers and acquisitions, in order to improve customer service, reduce downtime, and improve statement on-time delivery and overnight batch processing while reducing expenses.

Jaludi's firsthand experience has enabled him to fully understand

and embrace the ways process improvement, change management, and corporate culture are critical factors in determining how an organization can efficiently address and react to rapid changes in the business environment. The lessons learned during those 28 years are the genesis of this book, which focuses on the concept of process improvement, how to implement change and innovation, and the role of leadership in making those crucial elements of success an integral part of the corporate culture.

Made in the USA
Charleston, SC
03 January 2015